THE NERDY PARENT'S GUIDE TO RAISING A NERDY CHILD

An Unofficial Parenting Guide

LEO MURPHY

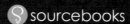 sourcebooks

All original art is copyright © 2018 by Sourcebooks, Inc.

Cover and internal design © 2018 by Sourcebooks, Inc.

Cover design by Timothy O'Donnell

Cover and internal illustrations by Sonia Liao: pages v, vi, vii, 1, 3-16, 21-23, 26, 27, 30, 31, 33-37, 39, 42-44, 47, 50, 52, 66, 68, 71, 73-77, 88, 90, 91, 96, 108, 109, 116, 119, 124, 130

Stock images © Freepik, Shutterstock: page 1, Nikolaeva/Shutterstock; page 17, Maria Kuza/Shutterstock; page 25, Aleks Melnik; page 38, RLRRLRLL/Shutterstock; page 41, Eireen Z/Shutterstock, Franzi/Shutterstock, ta_samaya/Shutterstock, owatta/Shutterstock; page 45, KateMacate/Shutterstock; page 52, Jivopira/Shutterstock; page 53, Bekki Schwartz/Shutterstock; page 55, Sopelkin/Shutterstock, Evgenia Prokhorenko/Shutterstock, kristinblack/Shutterstock; page 56, Arak Rattanawijittakorn/Shutterstock; page 60, Jiripravda/Shutterstock, Olga_Angelloz/Shutterstock; pages 64-65, derGriza/Shutterstock; pages 66-67, RATOCA/Shutterstock; page 71, Domira/Shutterstock Piotr Urakau/Shutterstock; page 80, zhekakopylov/Shutterstock; page 81, primiaou/Shutterstock; page 83, ksusha Dusmikeeva/Shutterstock, exile_artist/Shutterstock, Panuwatcch/Shutterstock; pages 86-87, owatta/Shutterstock; page 103, cetus/Shutterstock; page 105, Inga Maya/Shutterstock; page 106, hchjjl/Shutterstock, 107, Artem Twin/Shutterstock; page 110, mhatzapa/Shutterstock; pages 112-113, Macrovector/Shutterstock; page 115, kasha_malasha/Shutterstock, Arak Rattanawijittakorn/Shutterstock.

Sourcebooks and the colophon are registered trademarks of Sourcebooks, Inc.

All rights reserved. No part of this book may be reproduced in any form or by any electronic or mechanical means including information storage and retrieval systems—except in the case of brief quotations embodied in critical articles or reviews—without permission in writing from its publisher, Sourcebooks, Inc.

This book is an independent publication, not associated with, authorized, or endorsed by any person or entity affiliated with the respective brand holders mentioned herein, and is further intended as nonfiction, for reference and identification purposes only. All brand names and product names used in this book are trademarks, registered trademarks, or trade names of their respective holders. Sourcebooks, Inc., is not associated with any product or vendor in this book.

All activities in this book are to be conducted with appropriate adult supervision. Care must be taken by parents and guardians to select activities that are appropriate for the age of the children. The author and the publisher shall have neither liability nor responsibility to any person or entity with respect to any mishaps or damage caused, or alleged to be caused, directly or indirectly by the information contained in this book.

Published by Sourcebooks, Inc.

P.O. Box 4410, Naperville, Illinois 60563–4410

(630) 961-3900

Fax: (630) 961-2168

sourcebooks.com

Printed and bound in China.

PP 10 9 8 7 6 5 4 3 2 1

CONTENTS

HOW TO USE THIS BOOK

Before you flip to your favorite fandom's chapter and wonder why there isn't the highest level of content possible about your beloved franchise and this book gets labeled with fake nerd status…let's talk about what this book is for! As fellow Nerd Parents, our goal is for you to use this book to get your kiddo just as excited about geeky things as you were as a kid and continue to be excited about as an adult! We are by no means telling you to read *A Game of Thrones* to a toddler…but if you want to try and get your toddler into fantasy books before he or she can read, we have some suggested activities, crafts, and recipes to get your kid interacting with your fandom as early as possible!

The summaries and suggested starter comics, movies, and books in this work were intentionally chosen because they are the most mainstream options out there. Every fandom and franchise mentioned in the book has enough material—and certainly enough geek fun—that we could have made a book for each one! Our dream with this guide was not to be all encompassing but rather to introduce you to as many fun nerdy things as possible. We also wanted to create a book you can pull out and flip through with your children—hopefully with their own suggestions on where to start crafting, reading, and watching based on what they see on the page! So, start sharing the love and making an army of minions... and may the Force be with you.

INTRODUCTION: CREATING A FAN

There's something about the stories we read and watch as children that makes them more meaningful than any other stories we find at any other time in our lives. When we are young, our imaginations run free; they aren't weighed down by the realities and responsibilities of adulthood, not tethered by modesty, not limited by

time. It is for this reason that children find it so easy to believe in these alternate worlds, and they are so ready to be drawn into make-believe adventures.

That's what being a nerd is all about: immersing yourself in the fantasy. It's real to you, and it's a world you love. You acted out scenes, you created new stories of your own with those characters, you spoke their language, and you followed their customs as a part of your everyday life as a kid. Those stories shaped your childhood: you had the movie posters on your wall and the action figures on your shelf. You knew the movies and books by heart.

Now, as an adult, those stories are still important to you, if not more so, because they are some of the best memories of your childhood; some of the characters were your best friends, your greatest heroes. And they mean as much to you today as they did back then.

As a parent, now you can share that love of those stories. You can give the gift of these great stories that were so exciting, awe-inspiring, and life changing for you as a kid. And most importantly, you can share something in common: a love of these fantasy worlds. When you read these books, you'll remember just how awesome these worlds are and rediscover the love you had for them when you were a nerdy kid!

FANTASY

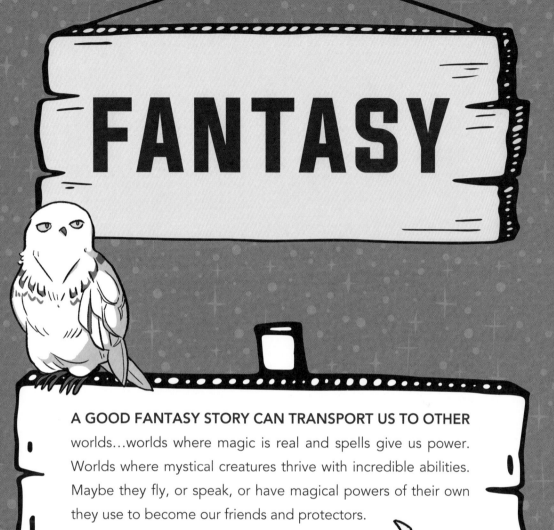

A GOOD FANTASY STORY CAN TRANSPORT US TO OTHER worlds…worlds where magic is real and spells give us power. Worlds where mystical creatures thrive with incredible abilities. Maybe they fly, or speak, or have magical powers of their own they use to become our friends and protectors.

Inevitably, some creatures in a fantasy world will try to use their powers for evil and to dominate and inflict rule over all who live there. But there is also good in these worlds. There are those who would protect and defend the beauty and balance that makes their world such a wondrous and amazing place. Thus, epic stories are born.

HARRY POTTER

"We do not need magic to change the world. We carry all the power we need inside ourselves already. We have the power to imagine better."

—J.K. ROWLING

When J.K. Rowling wrote the Harry Potter series, she created a world that became a phenomenon for millions of people, and it continues to be to this day. The Hogwarts School of Witchcraft and Wizardry was a school we all wanted to attend. We were enamored with the spells, wands, fantastical creatures, potions, moving staircases, and living paintings. If only our own school were as magical as Hogwarts! There, the education of young wizards and witches is a struggle between good and evil and the very lives of even the children are at stake.

The seven original novels of the Harry Potter series are now considered a cornerstone of young adult literature, crossing genres and age ranges in a way that had never been done before. The series starts with Harry and his class at age eleven, and the first three books read like fun middle-grade adventure stories. Books four through seven read more like darker YA novels. The series faced some criticism for gradually getting darker than it started, but it was actually

By the time the final book came out, it sold eleven million copies within 24 hours!

this evolution that made the series so successful. The series, its characters, and its themes all matured and evolved at the same rate as the readers, ensuring readers wouldn't outgrow the series. Readers literally grew up with the characters over nearly a decade of their most formative years. This coming-of-age for the series as a whole is one of the many factors that made Harry Potter the bestselling book series of all time to date.

Likewise, if you start your **six- to eight-year-old children** with the first book in the series, *Harry Potter and the Sorcerer's Stone*, and tackle a new book and movie each year, they will be age-appropriate by the time you reach the fourth book. The films follow the same pattern (and names!) as the book series, with the final book being split between two films, *Harry Potter and the Deathly Hallows: Part 1* and *Harry Potter and the Deathly Hallows: Part 2.*

Books and Films

1

Harry Potter and the Sorcerer's Stone—published 1997 (also a film released in 2001, rated PG)—Book one introduces the young orphan Harry to the wondrous Hogwarts School of Witchcraft and Wizardry. Harry meets his two stalwart friends for the rest of the series, Ron Weasley and Hermione Granger. In this book, Harry first learns of the evil wizard Voldemort, who seeks to return to a mortal form.

2

Harry Potter and the Chamber of Secrets—1998 (also a film released in 2002, rated PG)—In their second year at Hogwarts, Harry and his friends must solve the fifty-year-old mystery of an evil force that is turning students at Hogwarts to stone.

3

Harry Potter and the Prisoner of Azkaban—1999 (also a film released in 2004, rated PG)—The notorious madman Sirius Black has escaped the wizarding world's highest-security prison, Azkaban, and Harry is dogged by foreboding omens that Black is coming for him.

4

Harry Potter and the Goblet of Fire—2000 (also a film released in 2005, rated PG-13)—Now fourteen, Harry is a skilled Quidditch player, has his established group of friends, and is looking forward to watching his school represent in the international Triwizard Tournament...until he is entered as an unwitting fourth participant. This ostracizes him from his friends who believe he cheated to gain entry into the competition and steal the glory for himself. The end of this book marks a shift in tone and

4   complexity, moving from the travails of childhood and the shadow of an uncertain threat to heavier themes of death, libel, prejudice, and open conflict with Voldemort.

5   *Harry Potter and the Order of the Phoenix*—2003 (also a film released in 2007, rated PG-13)—Voldemort has returned, but the minister for magic denies this out of fear, seeking to avoid dealing with public panic. In response, Hogwarts Headmaster Dumbledore assembles the Order of the Phoenix, a secret society formed to defend against Voldemort and his followers, the Death Eaters. Harry discovers a prophecy that could be the key to defeating Voldemort.

6   *Harry Potter and the Half-Blood Prince*—2005 (also a film released in 2009, rated PG)—With Voldemort's return made public at the end of book five, Voldemort begins waging open war against wizards and Muggles alike. Relatively protected at Hogwarts, Harry begins taking private lessons with Dumbledore to protect his mind against Voldemort, and he learns of the existence of Horcruxes.

7   *Harry Potter and the Deathly Hallows*—2007 (also two films released in 2010 and 2011, both rated PG-13)—Hogwarts is no longer safe for enemies of Voldemort, who gained control over the Ministry of Magic in the previous book. Harry, Ron, and Hermione go on the run to track down all the Horcruxes and destroy them, the key to ultimately defeating Voldemort. This culminates in the Battle of Hogwarts, a bittersweet but worthwhile conclusion to the series.

Sorting Ceremony

A particularly fun way to introduce your kids to Hogwarts and the Harry Potter universe is to sort them according to the four houses of Hogwarts. Based on the characteristics of each house, which house will your little witch or wizard be placed in?

Materials

- A pointed hat
- A stool
- This book

1   Sit your child on a stool and place the sorting hat on their head. Then, read out the following descriptions and ask your child to decide which house sounds like it would be the best for them!

GRYFFINDOR—With a lion on its scarlet and gold crest, this house values courage and honor above all. A Gryffindor must be able to make bold choices in the face of great opposition.

HUFFLEPUFF—A badger adorns its yellow and black crest. This house

values persistence, hard work, fair play, and dedication to whatever chosen task is being undertaken.

RAVENCLAW—The eagle graces its bronze and blue crest. This house welcomes those who have a ready mind and value wit, wisdom, and learning.

SLYTHERIN—The serpent appears on its green and silver crest. Slytherin house values ambition, cunning, and resourcefulness.

2   While it's not strictly canon, encourage children to play and combine houses (Gryffin-claw! Slyther-puff!) when trying to best identify where loyalties lie. As Harry learned for himself, in those instances the child can decide their own fate.

INTRODUCTION TO THE CHARACTERS

Muggles or "no-majs" alike marvel at the rich characters that populate the wonderful world J.K. Rowling created. Hogwarts School of Witchcraft and Wizardry is the background for the majority of the series and connects many of the main characters.

Students

HARRY POTTER—Orphaned when Voldemort murdered his parents as a baby, Harry grows up in a Muggle (non-magical) household, not knowing he is a wizard until his eleventh birthday. After learning his destiny is to defeat Voldemort, he must gather the courage to make great sacrifices with the help of his friends.

HERMIONE GRANGER—At first a timid and studious girl, often correcting her friends' mistakes, Hermione becomes one of the most gifted witches of her generation and one of Harry's most trusted friends and allies.

RON WEASLEY—From a large family of wizards, Ron is the first friend Harry makes at Hogwarts. Often the one being corrected by Hermione, he is not the greatest wizard, or the best student, but he is truly a great friend.

FRED AND GEORGE WEASLEY—Ron's older, twin brothers, seemingly two halves of the same person, clever and mischievous, their playful deception brings them trouble, but it comes in handy when danger is near.

NEVILLE LONGBOTTOM—Tall and clumsy, better with plants than he is with people, Neville begins his journey as an awkward and odd child, but he grows into a strong and capable student and true friend.

GINNY WEASLEY—The only Weasley sister, she is shy but strong to the point of being stubborn; she is also just as passionate and kind.

LUNA LOVEGOOD—Quirky and creative. Some think she's downright crazy. Peaceful, thoughtful, and curious, she always on the side of good. Her gift of knowing odd facts sometimes even saves the day.

DRACO MALFOY—Son of a proud family of wizards and a strong believer in only teaching magic to wizards of pure blood, Draco's hostility toward unpopular students makes him a bully as well as Harry's rival.

VINCENT CRABBE & GREGORY GOYLE—The muscle to Malfoy's mind, these two young wizards follow Malfoy wherever he goes, creating a trio of friends who all share a mean streak and tend to oppose anything Harry and his own friends are up to.

Professors & Alumni

ALBUS DUMBLEDORE—Headmaster of Hogwarts School of Witchcraft and Wizardry and considered the greatest wizard of his time.

SEVERUS SNAPE—Head of Slytherin House and strict Potions Master, his motives and antagonism toward Harry are a mystery for most of the series.

MINERVA MCGONAGALL—Head of Gryffindor House, Transfiguration teacher, and later headmistress of Hogwarts, she adheres to the rules at every turn, but she would protect her beloved students at any cost.

RUBEUS HAGRID—Half-giant keeper of keys and grounds at Hogwarts, and later the Care of Magical Creatures professor, he is huge, strong, gentle, and a staunch ally of Dumbledore.

SIRIUS BLACK—Thought to be a madman, Sirius spent years in Azkaban Prison, but his family history and true nature reveal a very different man as the saga unfolds.

REMUS LUPIN—The Defense Against the Dark Arts teacher in *Harry Potter and the Prisoner of Azkaban*, Lupin is a fast favorite for Harry and his friends, bonding to the group and revealing secrets to the trio even after his time at Hogwarts comes to a close.

ARTHUR WEASLEY—Head of the Weasley household, Arthur works for the Ministry of Magic as the Head of the Misuse of Muggle Artifacts—an ideal title as he himself is charmed to the point of obsession with Muggle society.

MOLLY WEASLEY—The no-nonsense matriarch of the Weasley family, Molly Weasley has not only raised all of her own redheaded children but seemingly from the moment she met him, taken Harry in as well.

LUCIUS MALFOY—Draco's father, a known supporter of the dark arts and formerly suspected to be a Death Eater; he is loyal to Lord Voldemort.

LORD VOLDEMORT—a.k.a. Tom Riddle, a.k.a He-Who-Must-Not-Be-Named, Voldemort is the primary antagonist throughout the series. He begins as a mere spirit whose only wish is to return to mortal form and take his revenge against Harry Potter, the Boy Who Lived.

How to Make a Wand

For those ready to begin their magical education, a wand is a must-have!

Materials

stick or chopstick, about 10 to 14 inches long

paint, various colors

paintbrush

hot glue gun

1   First, find a stick—either purchase something sleek from a craft store or pick one up from your yard, park, or natural habitat. Any strong stick will do, or even something as simple as a chopstick to get started on your own magic wand.

If your kids are really young, and you don't want them waving sticks around, then rolling up a sheet of paper at an angle, gluing it together, and filling the center with hot glue to make a more flexible "stick" will work.

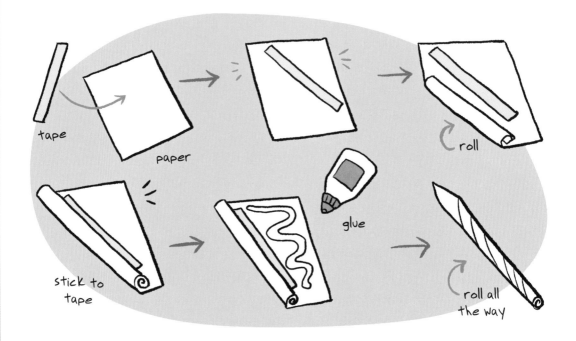

tape

paper

roll

stick to tape

glue

roll all the way

wait 20–30 minutes to dry

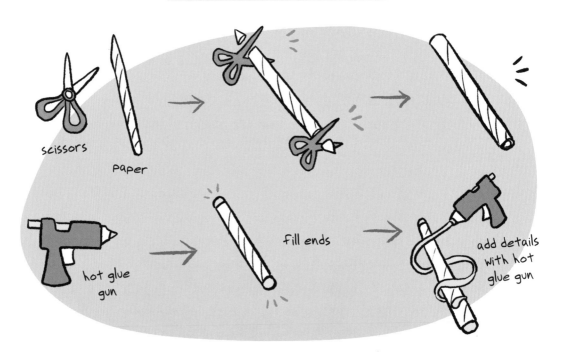

scissors

paper

hot glue gun

fill ends

add details with hot glue gun

base coat

spray paint

brush

acrylic paint

2   Paint the wand to resemble wood grain if you want a traditional wand, but don't stop your child from being creative! Any combination of colors will make your wand uniquely yours.

3   After the paint dries, you can use hot glue to make a swirling pattern on your wand to resemble decorative carving. Try several circles at the wide end and then a few lines traveling in a spiral up to the narrow end.

Water   +   acrylic paint   =   washy black

paint & dab with paper towel to get "old" effect

use a metallic marker to add final touches

4 Let dry, then paint the hot glue accent with silver or gold to let it stand out as a unique decoration for your wand.

5 Let it all set and dry, and you've got your very own Harry Potter magic wand! Have fun casting those spells! But be careful—you don't want to go turning any neighbor children or pets into hideous, unnatural creatures.

DONE!

How to Set Up Backyard Quidditch

Materials

- 6 Hula-Hoops
- 6 yardsticks or poles
- Tape
- 1 soccer ball

- 6 large foam balls
- 1 tennis ball or bouncy ball
- Broomstick, one for each player

1 Quidditch at Hogwarts consists of teams of seven players, but you can play with as many or as few as you have on hand. If you have an odd number of players, one can be a referee.

2 Find an open area to use as a playing field.

3 Tape Hula-Hoops to the yardsticks to create the goals. Set three on each side of the field at varying heights.

4 Each player should get a broomstick if possible. It's not necessary to play, but it does add to the fun!

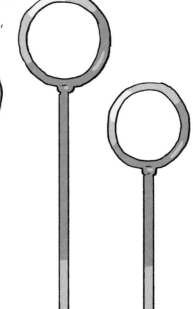

5   If you have seven players, each team has three chasers, two beaters, one keeper, and one seeker.

6   The chasers use the soccer ball as the quaffle. This is the ball that the chasers throw through the hoops to score goals. Only the chasers are allowed to handle the quaffle.

7   The beaters play offense. They use the smaller foam balls, called bludgers, to tag the opposing team's chasers and prevent them from scoring goals. If a chaser is tagged, he or she is out for a count of ten, and ten points are deducted from that team. After a ten-count, the chaser can resume play.

8   The keeper on each team is the goalie. The keeper guards the team's goals and attempt to deflect the quaffle from going through the hoops.

9   At some point during the game, the small bouncy ball should be secretly set or thrown somewhere, either by the referee or someone who isn't playing. This ball is called the snitch. In the films, the snitch flies around and is very difficult to find and get ahold of, so try to put the ball somewhere inconspicuous when the seeker isn't looking. The seeker's job is to find the snitch, and if the snitch is found, that team earns 150 points and ends the game. Whichever team has the most points at the end wins the game!

10 To maximize the fun, you can color your goals and the balls, and you can make any team uniforms you come up with; you can use just matching shirts or even matching capes!

PERCY JACKSON AND THE OLYMPIANS

"If my life is going to mean anything, I have to live it myself."

—SALLY JACKSON, *THE LIGHTNING THIEF*

Created by Rick Riordan, the mythic gods of ancient Greece come to life in this series of books. Gods fall in love with humans and create demigods. These human children are equipped with exceptional powers that they must learn to master and control. All the while, the gods argue and battle, causing great mischief and troubles for the young heroes who must use their powers to maintain order and peace in this world of gods and monsters.

Percy Jackson is a demigod, the son of the Greek god Poseidon and a human mother. At first he is unaware of his true identity, thinking he is just a normal kid. When Poseidon and Zeus begin to quarrel, Percy is thrust into peril that reveals the truth and sends him on many exciting adventures.

Grover Underwood is Percy's best friend. He is a satyr who is tasked with protecting Percy and eventually to deliver him safely to the training camp where he will learn to hone his innate battle skills, Camp Half-Blood.

Annabeth Chase is the daughter of the Greek goddess Athena and a human father. Although she is great in battle, she is very proud, though she becomes a loyal friend to Percy in his many adventures.

Books and Films

1 *The Lightning Thief*—2005 (also a film released in 2010, rated PG)—Percy realizes that the mythic Greek gods are real, and he must find who stole lightning from Zeus and return it before it is too late.

2 *The Sea of Monsters*—2006 (also a film released in 2013, rated PG)—Percy must rescue Grover from a monstrous cyclops and capture the Golden Fleece to save his training camp home.

3 *The Titan's Curse*—2007—Percy's friend Annabeth and the goddess Artemis have both been kidnapped, and Percy must quest to save his friends.

4 *The Battle of the Labyrinth*—2008—Percy must battle to save his home, Camp Half-Blood, from invasion by finding the mythic artifact Ariadne's string and keeping it from his enemies.

5 *The Last Olympian*—2009—A continuation of *The Battle of the Labyrinth*, Percy must use all of his training and gather all his friends to defend Mount Olympus.

This series is **fun for younger children**. It contains some frightening elements and battle action, but the content is never too intense for school-age children.

THE LORD OF THE RINGS

"Little by little, one travels far."

—J.R.R. TOLKIEN

Perhaps the most well-known and enduring fantasy world ever created, and credited as the inspiration for so many fantasy worlds created since, *The Lord of the Rings* is known far and wide as one of the greatest and most beloved epic fantasy sagas of all time.

The world of Middle-earth was created by J.R.R. Tolkien, who had been writing the series since 1917 when he published the first work in the series *The Hobbit* in 1937. *The Lord of the Rings* was written from 1937 to 1949 as a sequel to *The Hobbit*. It was originally meant to be one-volume of a two-volume set along with *The Silmarillion*, but his publisher dismissed the idea and published *The Lord of the Rings* in three volumes over the \course of a year in 1954. It is these three volumes that we are familiar with today.

During an age of men, elves, dwarves, hobbits, wizards, and orcs, the evil wizard Sauron seeks to rule the world. He consolidates all his power into one ring. It is the path of this ring and the war that rages to control it that sets the stage for the entire *LOTR* saga.

Books and Films

The Hobbit—1937 (also a film series released in 2012, 2013, and 2014, rated PG-13)—*The Hobbit* tells of the adventures of Bilbo Baggins and him finding the One Ring, a moment that sets the saga in motion. Bilbo is on a quest with the dwarves of Erebor to reclaim their lost city from the dreaded dragon Smaug, who can unleash unstoppable fire and death to anyone who opposes him.

1   *The Lord of the Rings: The Fellowship of the Ring*—1954 (also a film released in 2001, rated PG-13)—This volume introduces the characters and the backstory of the ring's creation and path over the last many thousands of years. We meet the Hobbits, Gandalf, Aragorn, and the rest of the characters who become the Fellowship, carry the ring to the evil land of Mordor, and cast the ring into the fires of Mount Doom.

2   *The Lord of the Rings: The Two Towers*—1954 (also a film released in 2002, rated PG-13)—The second volume depicts how the great wizard Saruman has sided with the evil of Sauron and seeks to obey his evil master by smashing the world of men. Meanwhile, with the Fellowship in pieces, Frodo and Sam, the two Hobbits who carry the ring, continue their quest to bring the ring to Mordor.

3   *The Lord of the Rings: The Return of the King*—1955 (also a film released in 2003, rated PG-13)—The evil forces are in full attack, the world of peaceful men is under siege, and it seems all hope is lost. Great battles are being fought for the lives of all who live in Middle-earth, all while Frodo and Sam come to the end of their great adventure to destroy the One Ring.

Though there have been animated versions of these stories in the past, in 2001 the definitive film series of this saga began. Produced and directed by Peter Jackson, and widely hailed as worthy of the great original stories, the films saw great success. The final film in the trilogy, *The Return of the King* won eleven Academy Awards, including Best Picture, Best Director, and Best Adapted Screenplay. With violence on-screen and involved, historical plotlines on page, this series is **best for young teens or mature preteens**.

INTRODUCTION TO THE CHARACTERS

The sheer range of species created by Tolkien will have any kid's imagination sparked! While the books are a bit dense for early readers and the films a bit violent, whimsy can be found in exploring the diverse characters and writing new fables in their stead. To set the stage, here are some of the main characters and fan favorites to explore.

GANDALF—Wizard—Immortal, wise, and known throughout Middle-earth, he goes by many names, has lived in many realms, and is among the first to recognize and investigate the rise of evil in the land.

BILBO BAGGINS—Hobbit—At first quiet and peaceful, he is drawn into adventure by Gandalf, who sees in him the potential for greatness.

Cozy hobbit hole! ↗

FRODO BAGGINS—Hobbit—Nephew of Bilbo and raised by him since the age of twelve, he becomes the central figure who plays the most crucial role in the effort by the forces of good to overcome evil in the Third Age of Middle-earth.

SAMWISE GAMGEE—Hobbit—Best friend to Frodo, and drawn into adventure and peril with him, where he demonstrates great loyalty and courage in the face of terrible danger.

MERIADOC BRANDYBUCK—Hobbit—Frodo's cousin and close friend who is mischievous and adventurous.

PEREGRIN TOOK—Hobbit—Frodo's cousin and best friend to Merry. He is fun, foolish, and often the unwitting cause of trouble for his friends.

ARAGORN—Descendant of Isildur and heir to the throne of Gondor, fearless and skilled with his sword, but he is also fearful of his legacy that has kept evil alive in the world in the form of the One Ring.

LEGOLAS—Elf—Prince of the Woodland Realm, he joins the Fellowship to see the Ring destroyed. His keen eyes and amazing skill with a bow help to see his friends through many dangers.

GIMLI—Dwarf—Proud and stubborn, his gruff nature and suspicion of elves is matched only by his bravery in battle and his skill with his axe.

BOROMIR—Human—Heir to the stewardship of Gondor in the absence of a king and captain in its great army, he serves his kingdom with honor, but demonstrates the flaws that have drawn other men to their doom.

FARAMIR—Human—Younger brother of Boromir and Captain of the Rangers of Ithilien, he possesses all the skill and loyalty that his family has for his kingdom, and his modest nature keeps him free of jealousy of his brother.

THÉODEN—Human—King of Rohan and noble servant of his people. He is overcome for a time by the powers of evil, and afterwards he feels a great need to redeem himself in the eyes of his ancestors.

ÉOWYN—Human—Shieldmaiden of Rohan, niece of Théoden, and selfless and brave in the face of great suffering by her people, many find great comfort in her leadership.

GALADRIEL—Elf—Great and powerful, immortal guardian of the Golden Wood, a ring-bearer herself with tremendous wisdom and loved by all.

ELROND—Elf—Leader of the Elven city of Rivendell and host of the White Council, his great wisdom leads to the founding of the Fellowship that would see evil struck from the world forever.

SARUMAN—Wizard—Leader of the order of Wizards and great in his power and influence, he finds power most important to him, which leads him down the path of evil.

SAURON—Necromancer, sorcerer—The most powerful incarnation of evil ever to live throughout the ages of man, he desires only to bend all the world to his will and command every living creature, great and small.

LORD OF THE LINGO

J.R.R. Tolkien was a professor of English language and literature at Oxford in England for much of his career. He loved mythology and ancient languages like Middle English and Welsh. It was a desire to make up a language that led to the Elven tongues spoken in *The Lord of the Rings*.

What is your name in Elvish?

MIDDLE-EARTH MORALS

Tolkien was deeply influenced by his devout Catholic faith. He created *The Lord of the Rings* saga during the years England struggled against the Nazis in World War II. Having endured World War I as a soldier, he served his country in World War II as a codebreaker; the work fascinated him and furthered his love of language interpretation and creation.

These influences can be seen in much of Tolkien's work. His work explores themes of good versus evil and a person's duty to defend home against invading hordes. He emphasizes the greatness and burden of royalty, and that even the most meek and mild among us, like Hobbits, can have a profound effect on the outcome of the most grand and epic struggles.

There are lessons here for children about what it means to be brave, to be selfless even when it is difficult, and about what it truly means to be a good person. You can reference these stories for your children when they have friends who need help, like when Sam helped Frodo through many dangers. If something becomes difficult, you can remind them of how Frodo kept on his path. If your child wants something they can't have, you can remind them of the times the truly good characters were offered the ring but didn't accept it because they knew they shouldn't have it.

There are even lessons about forgiveness, like when Boromir falls victim to the ring's power and threatens to hurt Frodo to take the ring for himself. The other members of the Fellowship forgive him because they understand that no one is perfect. And near the end of the saga, when all hope seems lost, Aragorn doesn't believe that Frodo failed. Even when times are tough for a child, there is always a silver lining.

The lessons in this book for your children are everywhere!

Elvish Lembas Bread

Here's an easy recipe to make your own lembas bread. It's slightly sweet and certainly filling! Just follow these instructions and be ready to set off on your own adventure with your fellowship companions!

Ingredients

- 1 cup butter, unsalted (2 sticks)
- ½ cup brown sugar
- 2 cups unbleached flour and additional flour for kneading
- ¼ tsp. salt
- ¼ tsp. cinnamon
- Honey for drizzling (to taste)

Instructions

1 Preheat oven to 325°F.

2 Allow butter to soften. Once at room temperature, combine butter, brown sugar, salt, and cinnamon until creamy and lump-free.

3 Add flour to the butter mixture and stir until incorporated.

4 On a clean, floured surface, knead dough until smooth—typically about 5 minutes. Add flour while kneading as necessary to prevent dough from sticking.

5 Using a rolling pin, roll your dough until it is approximately a quarter inch in thickness. Cut into approximately 4-inch squares, making sure to score with an "X" for true film authenticity.

6 Place squares onto a cookie sheet lined with parchment paper and bake for 20 to 25 minutes or until golden brown.

7 Let cool for 10 minutes, drizzle with honey to taste, and enjoy!

Camping Quest

Set up an overnight camping trip in the backyard or favored campsite.

Materials

- Tent
- LOTR books
- Homemade lembas bread
- Sleeping bags
- Other preferred camping materials

1   Go on a themed camping adventure and pretend you and your family members are characters from LOTR! Pack the books to read and bring lembas bread to snack on as you hike.

What is your quest?

GAME OF THRONES: A SONG OF ICE AND FIRE

"I am no ordinary woman. My dreams come true."

—DAENERYS TARGARYEN

In the epic fantasy world created by George R. R. Martin, the fictional lands of Westeros and Essos have many kingdoms, led by many dynasties. The clash of interests and wars among kingdoms over rule of the land dominates the lives of all who live there. The ultimate goal is to rule the world from the coveted Iron Throne.

The first book, *A Game of Thrones*, was published in 1996, and it was developed into an HBO series in 2011 that became a smash hit for adult audiences. These stories are definitely for mature audiences only. Yes, we agree, *Game of Thrones* **is NOT for children!** But for anyone who was captivated as a child by such worlds as Middle-earth in *The Lord of the Rings* (as George R.R. Martin was), this saga will capture the imagination of any grown-up fantasy geek or mature teen. In the meantime, we suggest starting kids off with watered-down storytelling of dragons and White Walkers, of triumph in battle and surviving the odds. *Game of Thrones* has many interweaving plotlines, some of which you can start introducing to your little warrior as soon as you think he or she is ready.

Books

1 *A Game of Thrones*—1996—The noble lands of Westeros and Essos are introduced, with many intertwining story lines involving the Seven Kingdoms of this fantastical realm.

2 *A Clash of Kings*—1999—The Seven Kingdoms of Westeros are at war. Meanwhile, to the north, the men of the Night's Watch defend their territory against the Wildlings.

3 *A Storm of Swords*—2000—With the Seven Kingdoms still at war, Joffrey and Stannis Baratheon both lay claim to the Iron Throne, while the Night's Watch is closer to war with the Wildlings.

4 *A Feast for Crows*—2005—The war of the Seven Kingdoms nears its end while a young Tommen Baratheon rules the Iron Throne under the eye of his mother, Cersei Lannister, amid much turmoil elsewhere.

5 *A Dance with Dragons*—2011—Jon Snow becomes Lord Commander of the Night's Watch, as many vie for their chance to sit on the Iron Throne and rule all of Westeros.

6 *The Winds of Winter*—TBD—The long-awaited sequel to *A Dance with Dragons* has long been outpaced by the HBO series and is ravenously waited for by fans. Supposedly, a seventh book will follow this work, but in the meantime, Martin is very hush-hush on an official release date and seems to be in no rush to finalize his series, releasing anthologies and short stories within the world of Westeros in the interim.

Make Your Own Dragon's Egg

Using a few simple crafting techniques, you too can become a mother (or father) of dragons!

Materials

- A craft store Styrofoam egg (come in a variety of sizes)
- Thumbtacks (standard metallic)
- Various nail polish colors (try for metallic hues in browns and blacks)
- Glitter
- Glitter glue and hot glue for added texture and scaling (optional)

1   After you have gathered your materials, you will need to make sure your Styrofoam egg is even and undented so you can assemble a pattern. The best path forward for symmetrical scales is to start by arranging your tacks in a layered spiral, starting at the base and working your way up to the top of the egg. Once your egg is completely covered in tacks, you should have an egg that resembles a metal dragon's!

2   To make your dragon's egg look like it was laid by a real dragon, color it with traditional dragon scaling. This is where your nail polish comes into play. Paint your egg using your nail polishes, layering wet coats with glitter for an extra dragon-y effect. You can use glitter glue and hot glue for extra authenticity, creating a leathery or cracked effect.

3   Once your dragon egg has been completed, let it dry overnight. Coat it the next morning with clear polish, let it dry for two more hours, and you too will be ready to claim your dragon parentage.

COMIC BOOKS

EVEN THOUGH THEY EXISTED AS far back as the nineteenth century and likely before it, the first phase of popular American comic books began with the publication Action Comics, the first comic to feature of Superman, in 1938, introduced by Jerry Siegel and Joe Shuster. With full-color spreads and action-filled pages, comic books became hugely popular. There weren't too many entertainment alternatives back then, so comic books became prized possessions, and they were as popular as any TV show or film today.

After stable popularity in the forties, the comic book genre exploded in the 1950s with the introduction of such icons as the Flash and others.

Then, in the 1970s, America was introduced to the greatness of Marvel Comics, who debuted the Fantastic Four and Spider-Man.

The classic form of comic books still exists today, with avid fans and collectors all over the world. The genre has given rise to subsets like "alternative" comics and graphic novels, and the modern age has brought us digital versions of our favorite characters and heroes.

POW!

MARVEL

THE AVENGERS

Comics

Every kid wants to be a superhero and have powers all their own! At least any NERD kid worth their salt. To get your kiddo started on the right path, explore the characters and comics recommended by fans. All of the films listed below are rated PG-13, and the comics deal with similar themes and plotlines—a good rating for these would be **for mature preteens or teenage readers**.

IRON MAN—After tech prodigy Tony Stark inherits his father's empire, he uses his weapon-making skills to build a supersuit to defend all those who need it.

What's *your* superhero accessory?

Recommended Reading:

Tales of Suspense—1963–1968

Iron Man, Volume 1–5—1968–2014

CAPTAIN AMERICA—During World War II, Steve Rogers volunteered to be injected with the Super Soldier Serum so he could save the world from the Nazis. Now, he saves the world from anything that would jeopardize peace.

Recommended Reading:

Comics #1 through #619—1941–2011

Captain America—Tales of Suspense, #59 through #99—1964–1968

Volumes 2–7, #2 through #13—1996–2014

Series to explore: Bucky, Hawkeye, Iron Man, Namor, Black Widow

All-New Captain America, #1 through #6—2015

THE INCREDIBLE HULK—After brilliant scientist Bruce Banner was accidentally exposed to gamma rays during experiments, his alter ego the Hulk was created, which he turns into when he gets angry (though he controls his rage to fight for good).

Recommended Reading:

The Incredible Hulk, #1 through #635—1962–2011

Tales to Astonish, #60 through #101—1964–1968

Volumes 2–4, #1 through #57—2008–2017

Indestructible Hulk, #1 through #20—2013–2014

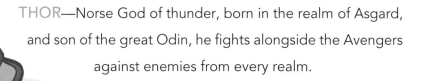

THOR—Norse God of thunder, born in the realm of Asgard, and son of the great Odin, he fights alongside the Avengers against enemies from every realm.

Recommended Reading:

Journey into Mystery, #83 through #655—1962–2013

Thor, #126 through #621—1966–2011

Volumes 2–4, #1 through #85—1998–2015

HAWKEYE—Enhanced vision and reflexes make Clint Barton incredibly skilled with a bow and arrow. Now trained for combat, he fights evil as one of the Avengers.

Recommended Reading:

Tales of Suspense, #57—1964

Tales of Suspense, #60 and #64—1964–1965

Avengers, Volume 1, #16—1965

BLACK WIDOW—Former Russian spy with enhanced abilities and a master of stealth, fighting, and seduction, she now works with the Avengers to right some of the wrongs in the world.

Recommended Reading:

Iron Man: Tales of Suspense, #52—1964

Avengers, #29—1966

Amazing Adventures, #1 through #8—1970–1971

Daredevil, #81 through #124—1971–1975

Marvel Fanfare, #10 through #13—1983–1984

Journey into Mystery, #517 through #519—1998

VISION—A robotic machine capable of feelings and empathy, he was created by Tony Stark and Bruce Banner as the ultimate defense against evil.

Recommended Reading:

Marvel Mystery Comics, #13—1940

Avengers, #57—1968

ANT-MAN—Burglar and tech expert Scott Lang stumbled on the Ant-Man suit made by Dr. Henry "Hank" Pym, and now he uses the power of the suit to help those in need.

Recommended Reading:

Tales to Astonish, #27, #37 through #48—1962

WASP—Janet van Dyne is the daughter of scientist Vernon van Dyne (who was Hank Pym's colleague). She uses Pym particles to shrink in size and fire blasts of energy, which she used to avenge her father and now fights for good.

Recommended Reading:

Tales to Astonish, #44—1963

DOCTOR STRANGE—A brain surgeon turned sorcerer, he is the great mystical protector of the world from dark magic.

Recommended Reading:

Strange Tales, #110—1963

GUARDIANS OF THE GALAXY—This group of unlikely heroes in the thirty-first-century team up to defend entire worlds from destruction.

Recommended Reading:

Marvel Super-Heroes, #18—1969

Guardians of the Galaxy, #1 through #62—1990–1995

All the Marvel comic books are filled with action and violence, but they are appropriate for children ages ten and up.

Films

"We all wish we had superpowers. We all wish we could do more than we can do."

—STAN LEE

The massive popularity of Marvel Comics in the 1970s found an equally massive fan base thirty years later with the release of films that captured the characters so masterfully and captivated audiences worldwide. From Captain America to Iron Man to Spider-Man to all the rest of these heroes, the stories told of the powers they wield and the villains they fight have revitalized the Marvel Universe for what will no doubt be years to come.

Where's Spider-Man? Check out pg. 43!

Hulk—2003—PG-13—Bruce Banner discovers his past and the incident that made him the Hulk. (Note, this title is debated among fans as the start of the first phase of the films or a standalone. This is included for your reference, consideration, or simply for you to explain to your protégé how wrong its inclusion is.)

The Incredible Hulk—2008—PG-13—Bruce Banner is forced out of hiding because the U.S. military is determined to copy his abilities for the sake of power and domination.

Iron Man—2008—PG-13—After suffering at the hands of terrorists, genius and playboy Tony Stark turns his weapons manufacturing empire into a force for good.

Iron Man 2—2010—PG-13—Tony faces Whiplash, a villain from his past with a score to settle.

Thor—2011—PG-13—The mighty god of thunder is banished to Earth where the ancient war he reignited follows him to the peril of the human race.

Captain America: The First Avenger—2011—PG-13—Steve Rogers volunteers to be injected with the Super Soldier Serum, and America's first superhero is born.

The Avengers—2012—PG-13—All the Avengers must put their differences aside and work together to save the world from Loki, the god of mischief, who seeks a realm of his own to rule.

Iron Man 3—2013—PG-13—The world is brought to a standstill by a global terrorist who takes Tony Stark's technology from him, forcing him to rely on himself without the Iron Man suit to save the world.

Thor: The Dark World—2013—PG-13—Thor must defend all Nine Realms of the universe, including his home of Asgard, from an ancient enemy that would see all the gods of Asgard defeated.

Guardians of the Galaxy—2014—PG-13—Brash space explorer Peter Quill stumbles onto a plot by the evil Ronan to gain the power to destroy worlds, and he must work with an unlikely group of heroes to save the galaxy from destruction.

Captain America: The Winter Soldier—2014—PG-13— Steve Rogers and the Avengers face a mysterious superhuman aiming to destroy the captain and his team.

Avengers: Age of Ultron—2015—PG-13—Hoping to bring peace to the entire planet, Tony Stark and Bruce Banner combine their brilliant minds to create a robot to defend the innocent, but their efforts instead create an enemy that they may never be able to defeat.

Ant-Man—2015—PG-13—A bright young man who has gone down the wrong path in life finds an amazing suit and the brilliant mind who created it, and he must use the technology to fight for good.

Captain America: Civil War—2016—PG-13—The Avengers are divided by what they each believe to be right, bringing them the most challenging enemy they've ever faced: each other.

Doctor Strange—2016—PG-13—A brilliant but arrogant brain surgeon who is forced to give up his practice is chosen to learn the mystical arts, and he becomes the reluctant wielder of great but very unscientific powers.

Guardians of the Galaxy Volume 2—2017—PG-13—Peter Quill discovers his true origins, finding his father and the root of some mysterious powers he may have. But the truth is not what it seems as Peter must decide the kind of man he is going to be.

Thor: Ragnarok—2017—PG-13—Thor in all his might and greatness still must struggle against his greatest and most powerful foe yet.

Black Panther—2018—PG-13—When the fate of his kingdom becomes threatened by the outside world, the young King of Wakanda picks up his mantle as the Black Panther.

Avengers: Infinity War—2018—Not Yet Rated—The culmination of the Marvel Universe, bringing all the heroes together to face the dreaded Thanos, perhaps the greatest and most powerful evil in existence.

WHICH AVENGER SHOULD YOUR CHILD BE FOR HALLOWEEN?

Refer to this list of hero archetypes to determine which Avenger your child could cosplay the best, and how to make homemade versions of their costumes!

THE GOD—Brave, strong, and heroic, kids who take after Thor need a tool to focus their powers. Set these kids up with their own fantasy weapon like Thor's lightning-wielding war hammer and let them build a world around it.

THE DO-GOODER— If your child always fights for the underdog, (or is the underdog themselves!), take a page out of Cap's book and sport America's red, white, and blue. Standing up for anyone in need is a cause all of us can embrace.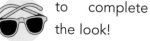

THE BEAST—Watch out! Your kid most aligns with a big, super-strong, and barely in control Hulk! If your child most aspires to being a huge monster on the loose, pad some muscles, tatter their clothing, and let the grunts start rumbling.

THE MASTER MECHANIC— Is your child a tinker and joker like Tony Stark? Technical, robotics-savvy, and cool, this kiddo is as quick with a comeback as a repulsor blast. Let your child build their own version of a super suit and watch the smile shine brighter than any reactor.

THE SPORTSMAN— Athletic and ambitious, your child may want to emulate the master marksman Hawkeye. All your child needs to emulate Clint Barton are black clothes, purple sunglasses, and a suction-cup bow to complete the look!

THE MASTER SPY— Stealthy and acrobatic, Black Widows are as graceful as they are dangerous. A ballerina-turned-fighter like Natasha Romanoff only needs black leggings and a long-sleeved black shirt.

COSPLAYING DEFINED BY MERRIAM-WEBSTER

Cosplay (noun cos·play \'käz-ˌplā, 'käs-): the activity or practice of dressing up as a character from a work of fiction (such as a comic book, video game, or television show)

"Sometimes people are miscast in life. They may appear to be dentists or clerks, but deep down they are actually fierce swordsmen or goddesses with devastating sex appeal. These true selves can emerge in the world of cosplay, the practice of impersonating characters from anime, manga, Japanese video games, and other realms of fiction."

—*MOTHER JONES*, NOVEMBER/DECEMBER 2007

SPIDER-MAN

"With great power comes great responsibility."

—BEN PARKER

A fan favorite since he slung his first web, Spider-Man is the superhero who captured so many imaginations and made genre fans of them in the first place. Created by Stan Lee and Steve Ditko, Spidey first appeared in the comic book *Amazing Fantasy* #15 in 1962. So successful was that one publication that it sparked its own series, *The Amazing Spider-Man*, debuting in 1963.

Spider-Man's alter ego is Peter Parker, an orphan being raised by his Aunt May and Uncle Ben in New York City. As a teenage high school student and nerdy bookworm, he has to deal with all the awkward struggles of adolescence. Having been bitten by a radioactive spider, he also must occasionally bear the burden of saving the city from the calamity of supervillains. Also amazing, he was the first teenage superhero not called "Boy," and not portrayed as a mere sidekick.

Films

Spider-Man—2002—PG-13—Peter Parker first develops his powers after being bitten by a genetically altered spider. He faces his first supervillain when the city is threatened by The Green Goblin.

Spider-Man 2—2004—PG-13—Peter has grown accustomed to his superpowers and is finding his way through the world, working with his brilliant scientific mind. This puts him into contact with Dr. Otto Octavius, who through his own experimental accident becomes the vile Doctor Octopus.

Spider-Man 3—2007—PG-13—This story finds Peter finally balancing his life between being a regular guy and a superhero, and he faces off against Sandman and Venom.

The Amazing Spider-Man—2012—PG-13—A retelling of the original story, we find Peter Parker back in high school and facing The Lizard, while trying to unravel the mystery of his father's past.

The Amazing Spider-Man 2—2014—PG-13—More scientific experimentation gone awry brings to bear the villain Electro; Peter continues to confront the demons of his past.

Captain America: Civil War—2016—PG-13—With the Avengers divided, Spider-Man must choose sides while he is pitted against some of the good guys.

Spider-Man: Homecoming—2017—PG-13—Now under the tutelage of Tony Stark, Peter faces supervillain Vulture.

Avengers: Infinity War—2018—PG-13—Spider-Man teams up with the Avengers, who are again united to fight the greatest threat to life they, or anyone, have ever faced.

Spider-Man-Style!

Spidey's take on capture the flag—on any landscape!

Materials

- Two flags
- Silly String

1 Create two teams, set two similar flags, and arm everyone with Silly String. The Silly String is Spider-Man's web, which can be slung at members of the other team.

2 Each team must try to capture the other team's flag and return it to their home turf.

3 Jump and leap! Sling your Silly String web at the other team! Duck and roll to avoid getting entangled in a web yourself! When team members get Silly-Stringed, they must stop running and wait for another team member to come and free them. They have to unstick the webbing from their body so they are freed to play again.

4 You can play up to a set number of points or amount of time to determine who wins. Your set amount of time might be short with all that leaping and rolling. It might be easy for Spidey, but probably not so much for us regular, nonradioactive fans!

THE DEFENDERS

"I know what I am... Who I am... And I'm not afraid."

—MATTHEW MURDOCK

Marvel's Defenders is a crime-fighting team that deals with themes for more mature audiences. This ragtag group recently came back into the public eye with their Netflix series in 2017, but being a superhero show doesn't make them kid friendly. The series on Netflix (both the individual superhero's series as well as the group series) deal with dark, more adult themes such as rape, violence, and gang-related crimes. A good rating for these would be **for mature teenage readers and viewers only**.

Comics and Films

DAREDEVIL—Comic debut 1964—Matt Murdock, blinded as a child, uses his heightened senses to fight crime on the gritty streets of New York City's Hell's Kitchen.

In 2015, the Netflix series *Daredevil* debuted with an awesome retelling of the dark world of Hell's Kitchen and Murdock's fight to defend the innocent and punish those who keep the city in the grip of crime and unrest.

JESSICA JONES—Comic debut 2001—A car accident left her orphaned and super strong. After a short stint as the superhero Jewel, she gave up her secret identity and fights crime without a disguise.

Netflix also rebooted *Jessica Jones* in a hugely popular series in 2015. The show's success is what led to the production of the rest of the Netflix *Defenders* series.

LUKE CAGE—Comic debut 1972— Carl Lucas was raised in gang life on the streets of Harlem. While in prison, he volunteered for Super-Soldier experiments that gave him super strength and super durability. Now he uses his power to protect those he cares about.

    Netflix produced *Luke Cage*, a slight reimagining of the original *Luke Cage* comic, with a successful first season in 2016.

IRON FIST—Comic debut 1974—Danny Rand is a martial artist who can summon the power of his chi to wield the mystical force of the Iron Fist.

    As the final Marvel Defender to make it to a Netflix series in 2017, Iron Fist rounds out the group with an original story line.

X-MEN

Comics

The original X-Men comics ran from 1963 to 1968, and they have had several new publications and added characters that remain in print. The comic book series was one of the most popular and bestselling series of all time, and Marvel in many ways set a standard for how exciting and entertaining comic books could be. Even during a time when films and television were developing entertaining titles of their own—and there were many heroes on the big screen—these comic books still captivated fans by the millions. Note, all the films are rated PG-13 and the comics deal with similar themes and plotlines—a good rating for these would be **for mature preteens or teenage readers**.

PROFESSOR X—Comic debut 1963—Charles Francis Xavier, telepathic master-mind and leader of the X-Men, is a force for good in the world and often keeps his fellow mutants from going astray.

WOLVERINE—Comic debut 1974—Originally named James Howlett and now goes by the name Logan, Wolverine can heal from any wound and even slow down his aging. With an uncertain past and indestructible metal claws, he is a tortured soul; more than that, he is an antihero who is prone to anger when his friends are in danger.

MAGNETO—Comic debut 1963—Old friend to Professor X and one of the first mutants, he does not share the professor's optimism when it comes to men and mutants living in harmony together. He often tries to dominate the world of humans, putting him at odds with the professor and the X-Men.

CYCLOPS—Comic debut 1963—Scott Summers suffers from the mutation of an uncontrollable laser force that blasts from his eyes. He is able to stop the optic blasts using special lenses. Under the teaching of Professor X, Scott uses his mutation as an important member of the X-Men.

STORM—Comic debut 1975—Ororo Munroe is descended from an ancient line of African priestesses. After a troubled childhood, she was taken in by Professor X, who helped her see the good she could do and to hone her skill of controlling the weather.

THE BEAST—Comic debut 1963—Henry McCoy grew into his mutation as a fierce, blue-furred monster with super strength. With his superior mind and the wisdom of age, he has been able to use science and diplomacy as his primary weapons against villainy.

ROGUE—Comic debut 1981—Her uncontrollable power to take the life energy away from any living thing she touches leaves her with a lonely life. It was Professor X and the X-Men who finally gave her a place and a purpose.

Films

"Just because someone stumbles and loses their way, it doesn't mean they're lost forever. Sometimes we need a little help."

—CHARLES XAVIER

Since 2002, the original and immensely popular *X-Men* comics have been produced into a successful series of films. The films loosely follow the original comics, but they have spun off into their own cinematic plots—a great development for Marvel Universe fans who can't get enough of the characters' adventures.

X-Men—2002—PG-13—Professor X leads a school of mutant children, helping them control their powers and live in a world that is not yet ready for mutant kind.

X2: X-Men United—2003—PG-13—Magneto sets into motion a war against humans as he tries to dominate the world. The X-Men must stop him and defend the very humans who fear them.

X-Men: The Last Stand—2006—PG-13—Science has created a mutant cure that takes away all mutant powers, a proposition that not all mutants think is a cure at all.

X-Men Origins: Wolverine—2009—PG-13—This film looks at the mysterious life of Logan, from childhood to when he was equipped with his adamantium skeleton and claws.

X-Men: First Class—2011—PG-13—In this film, which covers the beginning of the X-Men saga, a young Professor X and Magneto at first work together at the height of the Cold War, while the world first learns of mutants and their powers.

The Wolverine—2013—PG-13—Logan heads to Japan to see an old friend from his distant past, and he ends up having to fight an unexpected battle.

X-Men: Days of Future Past—2014—PG-13—The X-Men meet their younger selves and must change the course of history or face being wiped from existence.

X-Men: Apocalypse—2016—PG-13—The X-Men discover the very first mutant, Apocalypse. Ancient and worshipped as a god, Apocalypse reemerges to regain his former world domination.

RATED M FOR MATURE MARVEL MUTANTS

These films are not appropriate for kids. Start them here when they are eighteen (or when you approve of corrupting your youth).

Logan—2017—R (Keep in mind—mature content here. This film is not for kids.) The year is 2029 and mutants are all but gone from the world. While caring for the aging Professor X, Logan stumbles on a girl quite like him, and he must revisit his own troubled past to help her.

Deadpool—2016—R **(Mature content! NOT for kids!)** Wade Wilson, a former Special Forces soldier and wisecracking gun-for-hire, volunteers for a radical experiment to save his life. It does, but it leaves him scarred and able to heal from any wound, except for the torture he was put through, for which he seeks revenge.

Deadpool 2—2018—**(Probably also mature content! And also probably NOT for kids!)** Our irreverent antihero is back for more, fighting bad guys and trying not to become one himself.

DC

> *"Once you choose hope, anything is possible."*
> —CHRISTOPHER REEVE

JUSTICE LEAGUE

The Justice League is DC's most famous heroes assembled to save us all. The team's seven original members include Superman, Batman, Aquaman, the Flash, Green Lantern, Martian Manhunter, and Wonder Woman, although the following comics only note those who also appear in the recent DC films. A note for young readers, all the films are rated PG or PG-13, and the comics deal with similar themes and plotlines—a good rating for these would be for **mature preteens or teenage readers**.

Comics

JUSTICE LEAGUE OF AMERICA—Comic debut 1960—Created by Gardner Fox in the comic series *The Brave and the Bold.*

SUPERMAN—Comic debut 1938—Created by Jerry Siegel and Joe Shuster and published in *Action Comics* for decades; relaunched as *The Adventures of Superman* in 1987.

Fan Favorites:

All-Star Superman, a twelve-issue series starting in 2005. The original series of comics is hugely popular but so valuable that you may have trouble finding them!

WONDER WOMAN—Comic debut 1941—Created by William Moulton Marston and Harry G. Peter, first appearing in *All-Star Comics.*

Fan Favorites:

The Golden Age Omnibus, Volume 1, Paradise Lost, Spirit of Truth, Gods and Mortals.

GREEN LANTERN—Comic debut 1940—Created by Bill Finger and Martin Nodell, first appearing in *All-American Comics.*

Fan Favorites:

Secret Origin, Emerald Twilight, Rebirth, The Sinestro Corps War, Volumes 1 and 2.

AQUAMAN—Comic debut 1941—Created by Paul Norris and Mort Weisinger, first appearing in *More Fun Comics*.

Fan Favorites:

American Tidal, Death of a Prince, Sword of Atlantis, Time and Tide.

Films

Despite the recent success of the Marvel Universe, no character franchise has ever been more widely or intensely loved as the DC Comics characters of the Justice League. Superman, Wonder Woman, 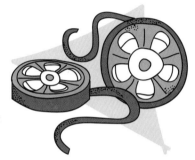 Aquaman, Green Lantern, and of course, Batman and Robin, have been favorites of fans worldwide from the earliest comic books of the twentieth century. And like all great comic book heroes, the films that followed were viewed in droves and loved by millions.

Superman—1978—PG—The Man of Steel grows up in rural Kansas and finds his way in the world as he discovers the origins of his seemingly limitless power, facing off against the human but insanely power-hungry Lex Luthor.

Superman II—1980—PG—Clark Kent gives up his superpowers for the love of Lois Lane, just before villains from his home planet of Krypton wreak havoc on planet Earth.

Superman III—1983—PG—Our hero must take on a power-hungry business-man with the help of an unprepared and bumbling computer hacker.

Superman IV: The Quest for Peace—1987—PG—Superman vows to rid the world of nuclear weapons just as the evil Lex Luthor escapes from prison, bent on revenge.

Superman Returns—2006—PG-13—Superman returns from a long disappearance, only to see how the world has gone on without him and how he must redeem himself while still dealing with the insane plotting of the evil Lex Luthor.

Jonah Hex—2010—PG-13 (slightly more mature content)—A gunslinger from the Old West finds himself in a supernatural fight for revenge against those who wronged him in life.

Green Lantern—2011—PG-13—Cocky test pilot Hal Jordan is chosen to join a team of protectors of the galaxy when he is given a ring of infinite power.

Man of Steel—2013—PG-13—A retelling of the Superman origin story, Clark Kent is raised on a Kansas farm and must discover his power before villains from his mysterious past threaten to destroy everything he holds dear.

Batman v Superman: Dawn of Justice—2016—PG-13—Batman and Superman are pitted against each other as Bruce Wayne worries about what could happen if Superman's unlimited powers are allowed to go unchecked.

Suicide Squad—2016—PG-13 (mature content)—A group of villains who have been captured and imprisoned are brought together to fight against the evil they know themselves all too well.

Wonder Woman—2017—PG-13—Diana, the Amazon princess and unmatched warrior, finds her idyllic life interrupted when a World War I pilot crashes on her secret island, forcing her to meet the world and help defend it against evil.

Justice League—2017—PG-13—All the heroes of the DC Comics world come together in the screen storytelling of the vastly popular comic series.

Where are all the best of the best Batman movies and comics? Check out pg. 56!

WHICH JUSTICE LEAGUE CHARACTER SHOULD YOUR CHILD BE FOR HALLOWEEN OR COSPLAYING?

THE GODDESS— Fighting for the helpless and demanding truth and justice for all, Wonder Woman is an inspiration to all. Deck your little Dianas out in bold colors for freedom and let them loose to empower the planet.

THE TOUGH GUY— When a child is found brooding over bedtime, you may have a Batman on your hands! Bruce Wayne elevated himself to superhero with his brilliant mind and his intolerance of injustice. Children looking to emulate the Dark Knight will be drawn to dark hues and cool gadgets to save the day.

THE OUTDOORSMAN— If your little superkid is consistently fighting for the planet and its inhabitants, they would undoubtedly have support from the Master of the Seas. Aquaman was raised to survive in the harshest of elements and able to communicate telepathically with animals.

THE LEADER— If your kid is a born leader, they may work to emulate Superman! Head of the Justice League, the Man of Steel is considered the most powerful superhero (whether this is true is up to you, fellow nerd), and a real good guy on top of all that. For children looking to inspire, simply add a red cape!

THE DREAMER—For Green Lantern, a ring of infinite power can take the imagination to new heights. If your child is constantly concocting new realms, daring creations, and unbelievable stories, creating your own version of a glowing ring can tap into their wildest adventures to date.

THE SPEEDSTER— If your child is anything like the Flash, you've got a bundle of energy on your hands! The Flash is capable of moving faster than the speed of light (or 670,616,629 miles per hour). Children who put the pedal to the metal need sneakers that have traction to match!

BATMAN

"It's not who I am underneath, but what I do that defines me."

—BATMAN

The Caped Crusader is a fan favorite despite his trademark gloom and doom. Orphaned at a young age, Bruce Wayne is a billionaire looking to save his city and clean up the streets by donning his vigilante gear and becoming Batman. Originally appearing on the small screen, Batman was a popular TV series through the fifties and sixties before making his big screen debut. While the original TV series' sanitized "POWS!" and "BAMS!" made for kid-friendly viewing, the comics themselves and the movies released to date are all **targeted for PG readers, ideally mature preteens and teens**.

Films

Batman—1989—PG-13—Tim Burton puts his twist on the origin story of the Caped Crusader and his battle with the Joker.

Batman Returns—1992—PG-13—This time, Tim Burton has the evil Penguin running for mayor of Gotham City, while Catwoman is causing trouble with her own crazy schemes.

Batman Forever—1995—PG-13—Joel Schumacher has Batman (Val Kilmer) team up with Robin (Chris O'Donnell) to battle Two-Face and The Riddler, both driven insane and wreaking havoc on Gotham City.

Batman & Robin—1997—This time it's George Clooney who battles Mr. Freeze and Poison Ivy for the fate of the innocent people of Gotham.

Catwoman—2004—Patience Phillips is a shy and demur woman who stumbles onto a corporate conspiracy. An accident turns her into the powerful and cunning Catwoman, her alter ego who is more than strong enough to bring the bad guys to their knees.

Batman Begins—2005—Christopher Nolan breathes new life into Batman. With Christian Bale as the dark and troubled hero, Batman's origin story is told in great detail, and he battles Gotham's criminal underworld.

The Dark Knight—2008—The Joker is back and crazier than ever as he spreads chaos around the city in one of the most acclaimed films of the series.

The Dark Knight Rises—2012—After years of hiding, Batman is back when no one else can save Gotham from the massive evil of Bane, who wants to turn Gotham to ashes at his feet.

"Riddle Me This!"

- Create a Batman-themed trivia game! Think you know all there is to know about Batman, the Justice League, and the villains they face? Then get some note cards and write questions on one side and the answers on the other.
- You can ask about characters, relationships, original story lines, and even production dates, directors, and stars of films! If you're a real DC Comics nerd, you might even know titles, numbers, dates, and the creators of the original comic book series. You could impress anyone with your nerd prowess!
- Here are some examples, but you too are the Batspert! Feel free to add your own!

Name all the film stars who played the role of Batman in order.
(answer: Adam West, Michael Keaton, Val Kilmer, George Clooney, Christian Bale, Ben Affleck)

What year did the original Batman television series first air?
(answer: 1966)

Who was the actor who played Robin in original television series alongside Adam West?
(answer: Burt Ward)

Who were the two actors to play Two-Face in the modern adaptations of the films?

(answer: Tommy Lee Jones and Aaron Eckhart)

What is Superman's father's name?

(answer: Jor-El, extra points if you spell it right!)

In what year did Two-Face first appear in the Batman comic?

(answer: 1942)

Who created the character of Two-Face:

(answer: Bill Finger and Bob Kane)

In what year did Superman first appear in a comic book?

(answer: 1938)

What were the names of Superman's Earth parents?

(answer: Jonathan and Martha Kent)

WHICH BATMAN CHARACTER SHOULD YOUR CHILD BE FOR HALLOWEEN OR COSPLAYING?

While any kid could be Batman for Halloween, sometimes it's more fun to be bad! Batman's villains are almost as famous as Batman himself—all of which are fun to emulate.

CATWOMAN—An antihero, this dark and powerful character is a fun character to dress up as for Halloween or cosplaying.

THE JOKER—With a bright costume and face makeup, the Joker is iconic and crazy.

HARLEY QUINN—A girl with a streetwise attitude, she's as done-up as the Joker.

PENGUIN—Wearing a tuxedo and physically small, this evil mastermind is imposing and spooky.

TWO-FACE—Part gangster, part deformed villain, he's the perfect balance between bad guy and scary monster.

THE RIDDLER—Head to toe in green with a mask and a top hat, this brilliant and cunning villain is visibly one of a kind.

BANE—Huge, muscle-bound, and scary with a military look and a mask over his face, he is a formidable figure to anyone who sees him!

SUICIDE SQUAD

"Don't forget, we're the bad guys."

—DEADSHOT

The Suicide Squad are bad guys who end up as unlikely heroes. First appearing in 1959 in Robert Kanigher and Ross Andru's *The Brave and the Bold* #25, they relaunched in their modern version in 1987 in John Ostrander, Len Wein, and John Byrne's *Legends* miniseries.

Created for slightly more mature audiences, and sometimes introducing new characters knowing they would be killed off, the *Suicide Squad* comics were popular not only for their awesome characters and action, but because their missions were not always successful. Readers never knew what was going to happen or who would survive—therefore both the recent movie and the comics should be **distributed only to mature teen audiences**.

With the members of the team often coming and going, the main characters were Deadshot, Harley Quinn, Captain Boomerang, El Diablo, Killer Croc, Katana, the Enchantress, and the Joker.

VERTIGO

"Everybody is special. Everybody is a hero, a lover, a fool, a villain. Everybody. Everybody has their story to tell."

—V

Created in 1993, Vertigo is an imprint of DC Comics designed to publish darker and more graphic works that fell outside DC's typical comics fare. **The violence and controversial subject matter typically equates these series with R-rated films.** Vertigo Comics has multiple award-winning series, with dark, intriguing stories and haunting illustrations. Comic books and series this imprint has published include:

Recommended Reading (for mature audiences):

Fables—Bill Willingham and Mark Buckingham's sprawling universe of fairy tale–inspired characters trying to live normal lives in modern-day New York City.

Hellblazer—Created by Alan Moore and Stephen R. Bissette, Hellblazer was Vertigo's longest-running series, featuring the morally ambiguous occult detective John Constantine. This series concluded in 2013, but the character of Constantine has continued in various DC comics, a film, and a TV show.

iZombie—Originally a comic book series created by Chris Roberson and Michael Allred, this series spawned the TV series of the same name, featuring a female zombie with the ability to absorb the memories of those whose brains she eats.

Preacher—Garth Ennis and Steve Dillon's religiously controversial series began as a comic book featuring Jesse Custer, a preacher in a small Texas town with a supernatural power of good and evil, and also became a TV series of the same name.

The Sandman—Neil Gaiman's masterpiece, this was one of the first graphic novels to ever become a New York Times bestseller. It tells the story of Dream of the Endless, a.k.a. Morpheus, and is famous for Gaiman's now trademark blend of mythology, history, and horror.

V for Vendetta—Created by Alan Moore and David Lloyd, this story depicts the now-iconic masked vigilante known as V, a theatrical anarchist revolutionary wreaking havoc on the fascist government of a dystopian Britain.

Y: The Last Man—The precursor to Brian K. Vaughan's Saga, this series was co-created with Pia Guerra. It focuses on escape artist Yorick Brown, the only man to survive the simultaneous death of all other male mammals on Earth, accompanied only by his pet monkey, Ampersand.

IMAGE COMICS

"Don't talk, think. That's a good rule of thumb for life."

—RICK GRIMES

Image Comics was created in 1992 as a platform for comics creators to have total decision-making authority over their work and to own their own material. A group of well-known artists from publishing giants Marvel and DC Comics had grown frustrated with the policies of those publications and decided to branch out on their own. The label has focused on the superhero genre, but the creative freedom given to the artists has led to such bestselling series as *Paper Girls*, *Savage Dragon*, *Invincible*, *Witchblade*, *The Darkness*, and *The Walking Dead*.

With artistic freedom, the label became known for a wide range of subject matter, as well as a compelling and ornate artistic style. The mature content and no-holds-barred stories captured the interest of adult readers who had grown up loving the comic books of their childhoods, creating an avid and loyal fan base that has made Image one of the most popular successful American comic book publishers of all time.

Recommended Reading (for mature audiences):

Saga—Brian K. Vaughan and Fiona Staples's magnum opus, held up as an exceptional model of everything modern comics can be, Saga is a literal epic featuring the lengths a mother and father from two different sides of an inter-planetary war will go to protect their daughter.

Spawn—Created by Todd McFarlane, this series featuring Al Simmons, a former special forces agent who makes a deal with the devil to return to Earth after his death as a vigilante to atone for own his evil acts in life.

Rat Queens—A wonderful fantasy series about a quartet of mercenaries that manages to simultaneously celebrate and subvert fantasy tropes, created by Kurtis J. Wiebe, Roc Upchurch, Stjepan Sejic, Tess Fowler, and Owen Gieni.

TOP COW PRODUCTIONS

"The extraordinary is in what we do, not who we are."

—LARA CROFT

A spin-off of Image Comics, Top Cow was founded in 1992 with Image, but it became independent in 1996. Focusing mainly of the fantasy genre, it brought with it such franchises as *Witchblade*, *The Darkness*, *Magdalena*, *Aphrodite IX*, and a few others. It also created new stories, such as *Fathom* and *Lara Croft Tomb Raider*.

In 2006, Top Cow agreed to create some crossover series with Marvel Comics, producing comic books featuring *Darkness* combined with *Wolverine* and *Witchblade* with *The Punisher*. They also did work for Marvel characters, such as *X-Men: Phoenix—Warsong*, *The New Avengers*, and *X-Men*.

The television, film, and video game adaptations of their many franchises have been met with a huge fan base and have enjoyed great success, with new titles being released year after year.

Top Cow also is one of the first major comics to offer its products online, publishing *Tomb Raider*, *The Darkness*, and *Witchblade* digitally for one dollar per issue and becoming among the first to take a huge step forward in the distribution of comics to the world.

Recommended Reading (for mature audiences):

Witchblade   *Lara Croft Tomb Raider*

The Darkness   *X-Men: Phoenix—Warsong*

Fathom

IDW PUBLISHING

"It's showtime, Synergy!"

—JEM AND THE HOLOGRAMS

Idea and Design Works, formed in 1999, was developed to create products having to do with video games, films, television series, and various board and card games. The comic book publishing branch of the company started in 2007.

The first publication effort from this group was *30 Days of Night*, which went on to become a popular and successful film. The company's second effort, *Popbot*, became an award-winning franchise.

IDW also publishes comics for a vast array of television series including: *Star Trek*, *CSI*, *Mars Attacks*, *Underworld*, *The Shield*, and *24*, among others. They also publish comics for the toy company Hasbro, such as *G.I. Joe* and *Transformers*, which has several series running simultaneously.

In 2008, they began a relationship with the franchise *Doctor Who*, owned by the British Broadcasting Company (BBC), which covered the long span of that show and the many doctors who have filled that role.

And there is an even broader range of characters now and in the future, some for younger audiences like My Little Pony and Jem. And a new partnership with Disney will bring on board all the Mickey Mouse characters and other Disney stories.

Recommended Reading (for mature audiences):

30 Days of Night	*Underworld*
Popbot	*The Shield*
Mars Attacks	*24*

Recommended Reading (for younger audiences):

Teenage Mutant Ninja Turtles	*My Little Pony*
Doctor Who	*Anything Mickey Mouse!*
Jem	

ANIME & MANGA

IN JAPAN, "ANIME" IS A TERM REFERRING TO ALL animation, and it translates close to the meaning of the general term "cartoons" in English. In the U.S., however, anime refers to a certain unique style of animation originating in Japan and characterized by a graphic hand-drawn aesthetic.

Anime's hallmarks are recognizable even to the casual observer. In character design: large, expressive eyes and spiky, brightly colored hair. In setting: breathtakingly detailed and imaginative. And in tone: heavily dramatic no matter the situation. It's easy to see why anime is a natural fit for the fantastical settings it is most known for, but in truth, anime is a diverse art form with a wide scope. One of the greatest pulls toward anime as a medium is that it delivers the same amount of passion and emotional engagement in a sci-fi epic determining the fate of the world as it does in a story about one plucky high school volleyball team.

Manga, in today's terms, is essentially the Japanese equivalent of American comic books, although it has a rich history originating in traditional Japanese art and is the source material for many anime series.

DRAGON BALL Z

"Over time I have grown stronger, my strength reaching new heights, but I have never gained more than the day you made it into my life."

—GOKU

Dragon Ball is a manga written and illustrated by Akira Toriyama. It was initially serialized in *Weekly Shonen Jump* magazine from 1984 to 1995, and it involved a boy named Goku and his quest for the seven magic items known as the Dragon Balls. The mystical orbs were purported to summon a wish-granting dragon when gathered, and so they attracted as many worthy folk as they did unsavory characters from the across the galaxy.

Dragon Ball Z was an anime adapted from the latter portion of the original *Dragon Ball* manga, and was the sequel to the *Dragon Ball* anime. *Dragon Ball Z* follows Goku into his adult life, as he raises his two sons, Gohan and Goten, and defends Earth from a wide array of intergalactic villains. A major component of the *Dragon Ball* lore is the training that Goku and later his sons undergo to master the power of their ancient race, the Saiyans, and defend Earth from those who would seek to conquer it. This involves many super-powered battles, but the violence is never too graphic and should be **appropriate for super Saiyans six and up**.

SAILOR MOON

"No matter how much you change, please don't forget there are people who care for you."

—SAILOR MOON

Sailor Moon is arguably the most popular and well-known shōjo series, meaning manga specifically aimed at a teenage female readership. (Likewise, shōnen, such as *Dragon Ball Z*, is aimed at a young male readership.) Originally serialized in a shōjo magazine published in Japan in 1991, *Sailor Moon* started as a fifty-two-chapter manga that was adapted in an anime that ran from 1992 to 1997. The story involves the main character Usagi Tsukino, a middle school girl who discovers she is Sailor Moon, the warrior destined to save Earth from the forces of evil. With the help of her talking cat Luna, Usagi awakens the other Sailor Scouts

and embarks on a quest to find the Legendary Silver Crystal before it falls into the hands of the evil Queen Beryl and the minions of the Dark Kingdom. A fantastical anime with preteen themes, this is **appropriate for Sailor Scouts six and up**.

Sailor Moon is one of the most well-known series in the popular subgenre of "magical girl anime," which typically feature a group of girls with magic powers that band 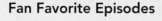 together for a shared goal. While the subgenre had its beginnings as early as 1953, *Sailor Moon* revitalized the genre and encouraged discussions about gender identity and gender roles.

Fan Favorite Episodes

"The Crybaby: Usagi's Beautiful Transformation"—season 1, episode 1— The iconic first episode in which Usagi meets Mamoru and Luna for the first time and discovers her destiny as Sailor Moon.

"The Shining Silver Crystal: The Moon Princess Appears"—season 1, episode 34—Usagi and Mamoru's banter comes to a head when their secret identities as Sailor Moon and Tuxedo Mask are revealed!

"The Sailor Soldiers Die! The Tragic Final Battle"—season 1, episodes 45, 46—In the culmination of the first season, all of the other sailor scouts bravely sacrifice themselves so that Usagi can continue alone. The power of her friendships and her love for Mamoru gives Usagi the courage to face her final battle, even if her friends are gone...or are they?

AVATAR: THE LAST AIRBENDER

"When we hit our lowest point, we are open to the greatest change."

—AVATAR AANG

Avatar: The Last Airbender is not, strictly speaking, an anime. American creators Bryan Konietzko and Michael Dante DiMartino cite Hayao Miyazaki's films as inspiration, but it is still more of an "Americanime"—a Japanese-influenced but American-produced show. However, Avatar is one of, if not *the* most significant works of animation to be produced by an American team in the last decade, and it merits an entry in any anime-related discussion.

Avatar is set in an Asian-inspired world in which some of the citizens are able to control one of the four elements through martial-arts-inspired skills known as "bending." Once a generation, one bender is born with the ability to control all four elements, and that person is known as the Avatar. The series focuses on twelve-year-old Avatar Aang's journey to master all four elements and bring peace to the four nations by defeating the ruthless Fire Lord and ending the Hundred Year War.

Critically and universally acclaimed and adored by fans, *Avatar: The Last Airbender* ran for three seasons from 2005 to 2008 on Nickelodeon, and it won numerous awards, including a Primetime Emmy Award. The series was so popular that it continues today in a series of comics published by Dark Horse Comics, picking up where the show left off, as well as in another TV series by Nickelodeon, picking up seventy years after the events of *Avatar: The Last Airbender*.

The sequel TV series, *The Legend of Korra*, aired from 2012 to 2014 in four seasons. The show focuses on the next Avatar in the Avatar cycle, Korra, a waterbender from the Southern Water Tribe, as she navigates the new and changing world after the defeat of the Fire Nation. With world-spanning adventure, clever, well-written humor, and visually stunning martial arts fighting but no graphic violence, *Avatar: The Last Airbender* is a perfect series for **viewers of all ages**. *The Legend of Korra* features more mature themes and teen characters that would be **suitable for kids ages ten and up**.

STUDIO GHIBLI

"Any woman is just as capable of being a hero as any man."

—HAYAO MIYAZAKI

Born in Japan in 1941, Hayao Miyazaki is a filmmaker and *mangaka*, or Japanese manga artist and writer. Miyazaki first started working in the field of animation in 1963, he and cofounded Studio Ghibli in 1985. He is widely considered one of the finest creators of anime films for children, and he is often called "the Walt Disney of Japan." Highly imaginative and stunningly animated, Miyazaki's films are highly regarded for their strong female characters and antiwar and pro-environment themes. Many of Miyazaki's films deal with similar themes but in vastly different ways. We recommend pre-watching his movies before watching with your little ones. While *My Neighbor Totoro*, *Kiki's Delivery Service*, and *Ponyo* are **sweet films for your little nerds of all ages**, *Princess*

Mononoke is a very mature look at the devastating cost of war on people and the environment, and is it recommended for **viewers at least ages thirteen and up**.

Films

The Castle of Cagliostro—1979—Suggested rating PG-13—This film tells the story of a gentleman thief. This film was Miyazaki's first turn as director, and it is credited as having a huge influence on much of animation, most notably for Pixar director John Lasseter.

Nausicaä of the Valley of the Wind—1984—PG—This film is based on Miyazaki's 1982 manga about a young princess who lives in a futuristic, post-apocalyptic world where she must master a huge weapon to save her people. This film was critically acclaimed as a masterpiece.

Castle in the Sky—1986—PG—A young boy and girl must keep a magic crystal out of the hands of military agents while they search for a legendary castle. This film is fantastical and futuristic, and it is revered as a classic.

My Neighbor Totoro—1988—G—Two young sisters befriend wood spirits in postwar Japan. Dubbed into English years later and released worldwide, this film's characters are now considered iconic.

Kiki's Delivery Service—1989—G—Adapted from the 1985 novel, thirteen-year-old witch Kiki uses her ability to fly on a broomstick to offer a delivery service. The story mirrors the real-life trials of adolescent girls.

Porco Rosso—1992—PG—A former World War I fighter ace, now bounty hunter, is cursed and transformed into an anthropomorphic pig who lives on to fight airborne pirates.

Princess Mononoke—1997—PG-13—Set in ancient Japan, this story follows a young prince and his country's battle between the gods of the forest and the humans who consume its resources. This film is widely considered a masterpiece.

Spirited Away—2001—PG—A ten-year-old girl enters a spirit world where her parents are cursed and she must work to find her way back to the human world. It won the Academy Award for Best Animated Feature, and it is considered one of the greatest animated films of all time.

Howl's Moving Castle—2004—PG—This story is set in a world where technology and magic meet. Sophie, a seemingly plain girl who turned into an old woman by a witch's curse, and Howl, a wizard with an uncertain path, are joined in resistance against fighting in a pointless war. This film was nominated for the Academy Award for Best Animated Feature.

Ponyo—2008—G—Abstractly inspired by *The Little Mermaid*, *Ponyo* follows the story of a fish named Ponyo who wants to become a human girl and live with a boy, Sōsuke, who rescued her from danger in the ocean.

The Secret World of Arrietty—2010—G—An animated retelling of the classic film *The Borrowers*, this film features a young adventurous Borrower girl, Arrietty, who wishes to explore the world of humans. She befriends the human boy Shō and tries to keep their small world secret.

The Wind Rises—2013—PG-13—Adapted from Miyazaki's manga of the same name, this story is a fictional account of the life of Jiro Horikoshi, the designer of a fighter plane used by the Japanese in World War II. Highly acclaimed and award winning, it was nominated for the Academy Award for Best Animated Feature and the Golden Globe for Best Foreign Language Film.

Kiki's Delivery Service

Pay it forward and deliver baked goods to a neighbor or friend!

"It doesn't really matter what color your dress is. What matters is the heart inside."

—KIKI

- Kiki is a young girl who can fly on a broom. She delivers baked goods for a kind baker who allows her to live there. Want to play like Kiki? Have fun with your child by doing some baking.

- You can pick up any bakery mix at the grocery store and bake according to the directions, or maybe you've got a favorite family recipe for cookies or cupcakes. Once they're ready, your child can deliver the baked goods to neighbors, "flying" on a broomstick as she goes!

- Despite what the movie may state, we think witches can be boys too! If your little boy loves the story, he can make deliveries of his own. There is nothing like paying it forward with baked goods.

SCIENCE FICTION

IMAGINE A FUTURE. ANY FUTURE YOU CAN DREAM OF. The technological advances—not magic, not supernatural, but based in speculative science. Science that could actually one day exist—space travel, time travel, wormholes, parallel universes, interaction with advanced alien creatures. All of it is possible, and all of it comes to life in science fiction.

Though advanced in its nature, science fiction is really as old as storytelling itself. For centuries, great minds have looked to the sky while contemplating answers to then-unanswerable questions. From myths like Greek gods throwing thunderbolts and dragging the sun across the sky, to scientific developments like those that occurred during the Age of Reason, science and fantasy have blurred together.

It was Jonathan Swift's *Gulliver's Travels* in 1726, Mary Shelley's *Frankenstein* in 1818, and others that began to shape the genre as we know it today. And at the turn of the twentieth century, H.G. Wells and Jules Verne created stories that pushed the limits of scientific imagination into the modern age.

STAR WARS

"A long time ago, in a galaxy far, far away..."

Perhaps the most iconic and beloved science fiction saga ever created, *Star Wars* began an era, defined a generation, and has become the standard by which all science fiction is measured. Despite moments of violence, this series is based around epic storytelling at a family-appropriate level, and **children six and up should have no problem becoming one with the Force**.

Films

The *Star Wars* films did not come out in chronological order, starting instead with what is now considered episode four. We recommend watching the films in order of release date, of which they are listed here.

Star Wars: Episode IV – A New Hope—1977—PG—The young Luke Skywalker, a lowly farmer on the planet Tatooine, is thrust into the perils of a rebellion against the evil Empire that rules the galaxy.

Star Wars: Episode V – The Empire Strikes Back—1980—PG—Deeply entrenched in the Rebellion and learning the ways of the Force, Luke must face his greatest fears and place his friends in great peril if he is to fulfill his destiny.

Star Wars: Episode VI – Return of the Jedi—1983—PG—Finally confronting his true past, Luke faces not only the dreaded Darth Vader, but also the great Emperor himself—the evil Sith Lord who will crush the Rebellion and see Luke turned to the dark side.

Star Wars: Episode I – The Phantom Menace—1999—PG—Years before the Empire ruled the galaxy, there was a peaceful and democratic republic called the Galactic Republic; the Jedi Order, masters of the Force, oversaw peace in the galaxy. A young Anakin Skywalker shows great potential with the Force, but destiny awaits.

Star Wars: Episode II – Attack of The Clones—2002—PG—Anakin is now a Padawan, a student of the Jedi Order. The Separatist faction tries to break away from the Republic and war rages, but a deeper evil silently rises to power.

Star Wars: Episode III – Revenge of the Sith—2005—PG-13—The Clone Wars rage for years, and the Republic stands on the brink of victory. A now older and more powerful Anakin is wiser and hardened by years of battle. But love and loss threaten Anakin, and the secret evil that manipulates him takes over, turning him to the dark side.

Star Wars: Episode VII – The Force Awakens—2015—A generation has passed. The Jedi Order is but a legend to most. Rey is a humble scavenger on the planet Jakku, but she is drawn into a conflict between the new Resistance and the military dictatorship of the First Order.

Star Wars: Episode VIII – The Last Jedi—2017—As the last of the Resistance flees that forces of the First Order, Rey and Kylo explore their connection with the Force, and Rey learns the truth of her parentage.

Star Wars: Episode IX—2019

Path of the Jedi or Sith...

Which path will you choose in the battle for the galaxy? Learn about the Jedi and the Sith and choose the dark side or the light side!

The Jedi

The Jedi were Force-sensitive beings who devoted their lives to studying the omnipresent energy of the Force, and they trained to protect the balance between good and evil. By harnessing the power of the Force and training with lightsabers, Jedi fought for peace and justice in the galaxy for thousands of generations.

For thousands of years, new Jedi trainees called younglings were brought to the Jedi Temple to learn about the balance in the Force and to be trained to serve the light. The younglings were then apprenticed to other Jedi as Padawans until they passed trials to become full-fledged Jedi Knights. Jedi who showed great skill could eventually become Masters. The title Grand Master was reserved for the oldest and wisest of the Jedi serving on the Jedi High Council, the ruling body of the Jedi Order and the guardians of the Galactic Republic.

Although the Jedi Order was eventually betrayed by the Sith, who orchestrated the Clone Wars and the Galactic Empire, two Jedi survived and continued training those in the ways of the Force...

- They value wisdom and devotion to the Force
- They revere to all life forms living in unity
- They hold a desire to use the special fighting skills of the lightsaber only to keep the peace

The Sith

The Sith were a faction of former Jedi who gave in to their deepest impulses and desires, and they devoted themselves to the dark side of the Force. They used negative emotions—anger, fear, and pain—to fuel their power and gain dominion over the galaxy.

Their power-hungry struggles led to division in their ranks, so after suffering a massive defeat by the Jedi, the Sith became much more focused on secrecy and survival rather than strength in numbers. The Sith Order carried on for a millennium through the Rule of Two, a philosophy that dictates there can only be two Sith Lords at a time, one master to embody the power of the dark side and an apprentice to crave that power. In an order that focused on strength through struggle, this ensured only the strongest survived.

Over time, their strength grew until they amassed the power to overthrow the Jedi Order, resulting in the Imperial Era. Once Luke Skywalker and the Rebel Alliance defeated the Empire, the Sith were believed to be wiped out, but in the vacuum the Empire left behind the First Order and Knights of Ren rose to power.

- They value strength above all else
- They are tenacious and formidable
- Their ultimate goal is unlimited power

An Elegant Weapon for a More Civilized Age

Make your own lightsaber!

Materials

- Wrapping paper tube
- Tape
- Marker, paint, or wrapping paper to decorate

1 You can start with a simple wrapping paper tube. Use tape, markers, and solid wrapping paper to add color. Draw any details on the handle that you can imagine to make it uniquely your own.

2 The color or the beam itself is determined by the color of the Kyber crystal in the heart of the lightsaber. Jedi used crystals from natural sources, and so their sabers came in a variety of natural colors, most often blue and green, but there have also been lightsabers in yellow, orange, purple, and black. Before 2015, it was believed that the Sith's red lightsabers were engineered from synthetic crystals. However, after 2015 and the release of *The Force Awakens*, the new canon revealed that the Sith actually steal lightsabers from slain Jedi. As the Sith bends the stolen lightsaber to their own will, the Kyber crystal within "bleeds" its color original color and turns red. A Kyber crystal that has been turned by a Sith can be healed and turns white.

3 Choose your path, and then choose your color!

INTRODUCTION TO THE CHARACTERS

The colorful characters that crop up in the Star Wars universe are completely unique—even at the molecular level! Aliens, robots, and of course humans are part of the core characters that fans are crazy for (in costume, fan fiction, and adoration alike).

LUKE SKYWALKER—Young and adventurous, he looks to the stars and knows he is meant for more than the life of a simple farmer. His adventures carry him across the galaxy and put him face-to-face with the greatest evil of his time.

OBI-WAN KENOBI—Wise and strong with the Force, he is perhaps the most well-known of all the Jedi. As a young man, he fights for democracy in the Clone Wars. When he is older, he faces old demons of his past.

PRINCESS LEIA ORGANA—The young princess, beautiful, brave, and bold, dares to stand against the Empire and fight for the Rebel Alliance and freedom for all.

HAN SOLO—A smuggler who is often on the wrong side of the law, there is no one cooler under pressure or quicker with a blaster than Han Solo.

CHEWBACCA—Huge, furry, and imposing, Chewbacca is a Wookiee warrior. His strength and bravery in battle are matched only by his loyalty to his friends.

DARTH VADER A.K.A. ANAKIN SKYWALKER—Bitter and evil and more machine than man, Darth Vader strikes fear in the hearts of all who cross his path.

EMPEROR PALPATINE—This black-robed Sith Master is evil incarnate. He's old and deformed, but he is possibly the most powerful user of the Force in the galaxy.

C-3PO—Formal and diplomatic, this protocol droid is never one to cause a fuss. Protocol and peaceful communication are his purpose.

R2-D2—Feisty and funny, this astromech droid shows unwavering loyalty to his human friends.

Books

There have been dozens of Star Wars books published over the years since the first movie premiered, each of them expanding on the saga in its own way. For fans who can't get enough Star Wars, here are some books in the Star Wars expanded universe we recommend checking out.

Recommended Reading:

Splinter of the Mind's Eye—1978

Heir to the Empire—1991

Dark Force Rising—1992

The Last Command—1993

The Truce at Bakura—1993

The Crystal Star—1994

Children of the Jedi—1995

Darksaber—1995

Shadows of the Empire—1996

Specter of the Past—1997

Wraith Squadron—1998

I, Jedi—1998

Vision of the Future—1998

The Bounty Hunter Wars—1999

Vector Prime—1999

Rogue Planet—2000

Darth Maul: Shadow Hunter—2001

Cloak of Deception—2001

Star by Star—2001

Traitor—2002

Tatooine Ghost—2003

Shatterpoint—2003

The Unifying Force—2003

Survivor's Quest—2004

The Cestus Deception—2004

MedStar I: Battle Surgeons—2004

Jedi Trial—2004

Labyrinth of Evil—2005

Dark Lord: The Rise of Darth
Vader—2005

Outbound Flight—2006

Bloodlines—2006

Darth Bane: Path of Destruction—2006

Allegiance—2007

Darth Bane: Rule of Two—2007

Fate of the Jedi: Outcast—2009

Death Troopers—2009

Darth Bane: Dynasty of Evil—2009

The Old Republic: Fatal Alliance—2010

The Old Republic: Revan—2011

Darth Plagueis—2012

Fate of the Jedi: Apocalypse—2012

A New Dawn—2014

Heir to the Jedi—2015

Lords of the Sith—2015

Dark Disciple—2015

Aftermath—2015

Lost Stars—2015

Aftermath: Life Debt—2016

Catalyst—2016

DOCTOR WHO

"I don't need a sword, because I am The Doctor, and this is my spoon."

—THE 12TH DOCTOR

Created in 1963, the TV show *Doctor Who* is about the adventures of the Time Lord from the planet Gallifrey who travels through time and space in his British police box of a spaceship called the TARDIS. This mind-bending series pushes the limits of series storytelling with its intelligent narrative and exciting adventures.

The series ran from 1963 to 1989, and had a successful rebirth in 2005. A goofy romp through space, this is **acceptable for all Whovians five and up**.

As a Time Lord, the Doctor has the ability to regenerate into a new physical form with a slightly different personality after events that normally result in death for a human. This gives the show virtually unlimited potential for new stories as different actors are able to step into the role.

To date, thirteen actors have played the Doctor, each with varying levels of popularity with fans. Which Doctor is YOUR favorite? As you can see from the table below, all have their wonderful quirks, but be sure to explain to your little Whovian why your Doctor is best!

Doctor #	Actor	Years Active	Description
1	William Hartnell	1963–1966	He may appear old and frail, but he is a cunning Time Lord and fierce opponent of any evil force he encounters.
2	Patrick Troughton	1966–1969	Outwardly lighthearted and witty, this Doctor hid some dark character elements and a brilliant scientific mind.
3	Jon Pertwee	1970–1974	Brave and bold, this Doctor was also deeply loyal to those he cared about.
4	Tom Baker	1974–1981	Happy, adventurous, and charming, this scarf-wearing Doctor was also brave, giving his life to save the universe.
5	Peter Davison	1982–1984	Fascinated with all things scientific, he loved a complicated challenge. He was also a compassionate and kind soul.
6	Colin Baker	1984–1986	Gregarious and outgoing, his actions were as loud and colorful as the bright clothes he wore.
7	Sylvester McCoy	1987–1989	A joyful and joking sort, he liked to clown around, but he was as slick and cunning as any Time Lord would be.

8	Paul McGann	1996	Because of the adventures he faced, he was more of a warrior. He was strong and brave; he needed to be to defeat his enemies.
The War Doctor	John Hurt	2013	Hardened from years of battle, this Doctor had some difficult choices to make. This Doctor was retroactively inserted between the Eighth and Ninth Doctors for the show's 50th anniversary special.
9	Christopher Eccleston	2005	Seemingly frivolous and carefree, this Doctor hid dark secrets about his past actions in the Time War.
10	David Tennant	2005–2010	Brilliant but sporadic, this Doctor battled a wide range of evil forces and was defiant to the end.
11	Matt Smith	2010–2013	Young and energetic, this Doctor repopularized bow ties and was even a sometimes romantic, but he still had the old soul of a Time Lord.
12	Peter Capaldi	2014–2017	Intelligent and serious, this Doctor was older and wiser, but he was always brave and compassionate.
13	Jodie Whittaker	2018-	The first female Doctor to appear in our known universe has fans ecstatic about new frontiers.

TARDIS Fort Building

Grab your companion and sonic screwdriver—it's time to explore all of time and space! TARDIS stands for "Time And Relative Dimension In Space." As its name implies, the TARDIS is the time-traveling spacecraft that the Doctor uses on his adventures. Here's how to build your own TARDIS and play your own version of Doctor Who.

1 Find a refrigerator box or something similar (you can also buy large boxes from moving companies or online). Cut a door so you can step inside. As the advanced science of the TARDIS allows the inside of the ship to be much bigger than it appears on the outside, you can create your own version of this effect by cutting out another door in the back. Place the box in front of a doorway in your house so you can walk through to another room, pretending this room is the inside of the TARDIS itself!

2 Paint your box police-box blue, and add the exterior details to the box. (See next page for more!)

3 Decorate the "inside." Set up a table in the room you're using as the inside of the TARDIS. You can set up the TARDIS's operating station with gadgets, buttons, levers, lights, and anything else you find. You're now ready to fly through time and space on your many great adventures! Beware of Weeping Angels, Daleks, and the Master!

Exterminate! Exterminate!

BUILD A TARDIS FORT

SUPPLIES NEEDED

scissors · paint · paintbrush · markers · large cardboard box

ALL SIDES ▶ REPEAT ALL STEPS FOR ALL SIDES OF THE BOX (EXCEPT TOP AND BOTTOM)

ZOOM IN ON TOP

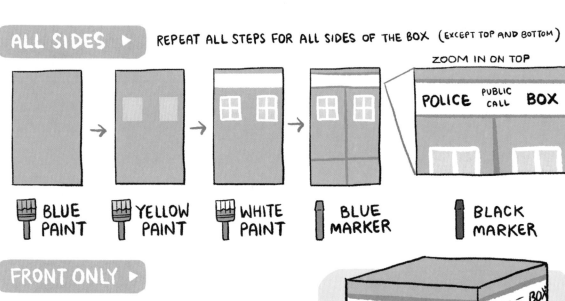

POLICE PUBLIC CALL BOX

🖌 BLUE PAINT → 🖌 YELLOW PAINT → 🖌 WHITE PAINT → BLUE MARKER → BLACK MARKER

FRONT ONLY ▶

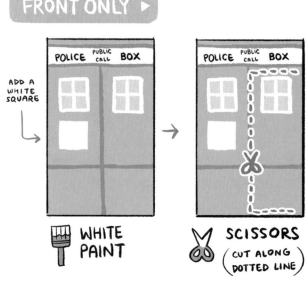

ADD A WHITE SQUARE

POLICE PUBLIC CALL BOX

🖌 WHITE PAINT → ✂ SCISSORS (CUT ALONG DOTTED LINE)

POLICE PUBLIC CALL BOX POLICE = BOX

DONE!

STAR TREK

"Space: the final frontier. These are the voyages of the Starship *Enterprise*. Its five-year mission: to explore strange new worlds, to seek out new life and new civilizations, to boldly go where no man has gone before."

—GENE RODDENBERRY,

STAR TREK INTRODUCTION

There is no science fiction world created that was more groundbreaking and progressive for its time than the original series of *Star Trek*. The crew of the starship *Enterprise*, who would "boldly go where no man has gone before," captivated a core audience that grew into one of the most loyal and devoted fan bases ever formed.

The adventures of the crew brought them to alien worlds and never-before-seen cultures, but the undertones of the stories often mirrored the contemporary social and political realities of the times in which they were filmed. The themes of class warfare, racism, religion, and human rights were all metaphorically tackled in these episodes, through brilliantly told stories with bold and clear undertones.

TV Series

Star Trek: The Original Series—Three seasons, 1966–1969—Created by Gene Roddenberry, the original television series debuted in 1966. Captain James T. Kirk, played by William Shatner, led the crew of the starship *Enterprise* on a long voyage of space exploration, representing the interstellar federal republic the United Federation of Planets.

Stark Trek: The Animated Series - Two seasons, 1973-1974 - Following the events of the Original Series, this fun animated reprisal had most of the stars from the original series lending their voices to their animated counterparts and won Star Trek it's first Emmy.

Star Trek: The Next Generation—Seven seasons, 1987–1994—Dated one century after the original series, Captain Jean-Luc Picard took the helm of the *Enterprise* in this new series. Sir Patrick Stewart played the role of Captain Jean-Luc Picard to great popularity, revitalizing the franchise.

Star Trek: Deep Space Nine—Seven seasons, 1993–1999—Taking place right after *TNG*, this series features Captain Benjamin Sisko and the crew aboard the titular space station, rather than aboard a starship.

Star Trek: Voyager—Seven seasons, 1995–2001—Featuring the first female commanding office in a leading role, *Voyager* features Captain Kathryn Janeway and her crew aboard the starship *Voyager*.

Star Trek: Enterprise—Four seasons, 2001–2005—A prequel to the original series, *Enterprise* took place in the years before the founding of the Federation.

Star Trek: Discovery—2017–Present—Premiering in 2017, this new series takes place roughly ten years before the events of the original series and promises the exciting early tensions between the newly formed United Federation of Planets and the warrior race of the Klingons. The leading character is Lieutenant Commander Michael Burnham, played by Sonequa Martin-Green, first officer aboard the starship *Discovery*.

Films

Star Trek: The Motion Picture—1979—G—After his first stint as captain of the *Enterprise* for the television series, Kirk retakes the captain's chair to investigate an alien force that is approaching Earth, with possible plans to destroy it.

Star Trek II: The Wrath of Khan—1982—PG—A continuation of a story from the television series, Kirk and his crew face an old enemy, Khan. A superhuman being, Khan is twisted with rage at the fate thrust upon him by Kirk, and who would do anything, even die, to exact his revenge.

Star Trek III: The Search for Spock—1984—PG—The consciousness of Spock lives on in Dr. McCoy, and the race to give Spock new life causes the characters to make great sacrifices.

Star Trek IV: The Voyage Home—1986—PG—A huge alien ship has entered the galaxy, headed for Earth and seeming to want to destroy it. Kirk and the crew must do what it takes to save Earth, which includes time travel back to the twentieth century, to much comic effect.

Star Trek V: The Final Frontier—1989—PG—The Great Barrier at the edge of space is investigated in this story, as Spock's half brother believes that God himself lies beyond this barrier.

Star Trek VI: The Undiscovered Country—1991—PG—In a surprising twist, the warrior world of Klingon is forced to seek peace with the United Federation of Planets, but no one is more suspicious of the intentions of the Klingons than Captain Kirk himself.

Star Trek: Generations—1994—PG—The original cast of *Star Trek* passes the torch to the new *Star Trek: The Next Generation* cast. Captain Picard meets Kirk, and they work together to battle a mad scientist who is seeking to bend all time and space to his will.

Star Trek: First Contact—1996—PG-13—In another time travel adventure, the crew of the *Enterprise* must go back in time to visit Earth of the past to save its future.

Star Trek: Insurrection—1998—PG—When a planet that serves as a fountain of youth, where its inhabitants never grow old or die, is discovered, it suddenly comes under attack, and the battle to save this idyllic world and its inhabitants ensues.

Star Trek: Nemesis—2002—PG-13—A Romulan leader, Shinzon, claims to be the genetic clone of Picard himself, and he seems to want to create peaceful ties with Picard and the Federation. Shinzon's true plans are slowly discovered, and real friends and enemies are revealed.

Star Trek—2009—PG-13—This reboot focuses on Captain Kirk's young life and entrance into Starfleet. At the helm of the *Enterprise*, Kirk sets off to explore new worlds with his intrepid crew.

Star Trek: Into Darkness—2013—PG-13—In this second film of the rebooted franchise, the brilliant superhuman Khan brings Kirk and his crew into hostile territory and causes destruction in an attempt to save his own crew and be free of the Federation.

Star Trek: Beyond—2016—PG-13—Kirk and the crew find themselves marooned on a foreign planet where they must fight a new alien race of beings to save themselves and millions of other innocent lives.

All the *Star Trek* films are appropriate for all ages, but with mild action, violence, and occasional mature content, parental guidance is suggested.

Books

The original TV series led to a series of books, twelve in all, written by James Blish from 1967 to 1977. They were simply titled *Star Trek 1* through *Star Trek 12*.

Starting in 1976, variant novels based on the Star Trek franchise were published, with almost twenty titles being published until 1994.

The New Voyages—1976

Spock, Messiah!—1976

The Price of the Phoenix—1977

Planet of Judgment—1977

The New Voyages 2—1978

Mudd's Angels—1978

Vulcan!—1978

The Starless World—1978

Trek to Madworld—1979

World Without End—1979

The Fate of the Phoenix—1979

Devil World—1979

Perry's Planet—1980

The Galactic Whirlpool—1980

Death's Angel—1981

Day of the Dove—1985

Mudd's Enterprise—1994

INTRODUCTION TO THE CHARACTERS

With its diverse band of space heroes, Star Trek prides itself on having the richest characters in any known galaxy. With main characters portrayed by people of color, Star Trek destroyed barriers at its time and portrayed a future with more diverse and hopeful backgrounds for our civilization to settle into. Kids would be thrilled to emulate any of the fan favorites, such as:

KIRK—No one is more fearless in battle, more charming in diplomacy, and more brazen in the face of danger as the legendary first captain of the *Enterprise*.

SPOCK—A half-Vulcan science officer, Spock lives his life in pure logic and intelligence, but he's fearless and skilled in battle.

UHURA—Smart and dignified, Lieutenant Uhura is the communications officer aboard the *Enterprise*. A role model for many, Uhura was the first African American woman on television in a nontraditional and nonstereotypical role.

DR. MCCOY—A brilliant doctor who is led by compassion and emotion, his goal is to save every sick or injured being he comes across in his adventures.

SCOTTY—Living in the engine room of the *Enterprise*, Scotty is the chief engineer of the starship. No one knows the technical layout and capabilities of his ship, as he communicates to his captain in his thick Scottish accent.

WORF—The first Klingon in Starfleet and a warrior by nature, this security officer has tamed his fighting spirit to work alongside his companions, until it is time to defend them from danger.

DATA—The most advanced cybernetic life-form ever created, Data is an endless source of information and knowledge, but so much like a child when it comes to emotions and friendships.

PICARD—A fan favorite captain of the *Enterprise*, Jean-Luc was a celebrated Starfleet officer, archaeologist, and diplomat.

INTERGALACTIC MORALS

The cultural impact of the Star Trek franchise simply cannot be overstated. As each crew faced never-before-encountered life-forms and alien cultures, fearlessness and diplomacy were always necessary. They illustrated a peaceful approach with a finger on the trigger.

The original series was action-packed and edgy for its time. Captain Kirk was bold and charismatic, ready for anything as he explored new worlds.

The next generation found a captain who was much more diplomatic and reserved in his nature, and this series was more complex and cerebral than the original.

But always, the theme of the story is that peace is the ultimate goal, that friendship prevails, and that being a good person in face of adversity is always the way to win.

Live Long and Prosper

Leonard Nimoy, the original Spock, claims he created the Vulcan salute as a variation of a prayer gesture from his Jewish faith as a child. Exactly how do you emulate this peaceful salute for yourself?

To create the Vulcan salute, put your hand up in a wave with your fingers straight and together, and then separate them between the ring and middle fingers.

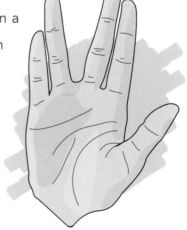

Used by Spock in the original series, the hand gesture is said to be both a greeting and a farewell salute from the Vulcan culture that conveys a message of peace and friendship.

BATTLESTAR GALACTICA

"There are those who believe that life here began out there, far across the universe, with tribes of humans who may have been the forefathers of the Egyptians, or the Toltecs, or the Mayans, that they may have been the architects of the Great Pyramids, or the lost civilizations of Lemuria or Atlantis. Some believe that there may yet be brothers of man who even now fight to survive—somewhere beyond the heavens!"

—PATRICK MACNEE,
BATTLESTAR GALACTICA INTRODUCTION

C reated by Glen A. Larson, *Battlestar Galactica* ran in 1978 and 1979 for one season and then for a revival season called *Galactica 1980* in 1980. Though dramatic and sometimes action-packed, the science fiction series is **appropriate for mature younger viewers, perhaps as young as ten**.

The story follows a ragtag military space fleet, fleeing across the stars from its robotic enemy, the Cylons. Their home planet destroyed, they seek a new world, a planet known only in legend as what may be the origin of their species: "A shining planet known as Earth."

The series was reimagined with much of its origin story in 2004 with great fan popularity and critical success. **This new series is intended for more mature audiences**.

A spin-off series, *Caprica*, ran for one season in 2010, which is also for more mature audiences.

THE HUNGER GAMES

"Hope is the only thing stronger than fear."

—SUZANNE COLLINS

In a tragic near-future world, the government has divided the country into twelve districts, and it rules over all the land with devastating power. Each year, every district must sacrifice a boy and a girl to what have come to be known as the Hunger Games, a cruel spectacle where children are forced to fight to the death in the name of their home district as a reminder to never again rise up against the Capitol. In the midst of this oppression, a girl, Katniss Everdeen, rises to stand for her district, and eventually for all those oppressed by the crushing rule of law.

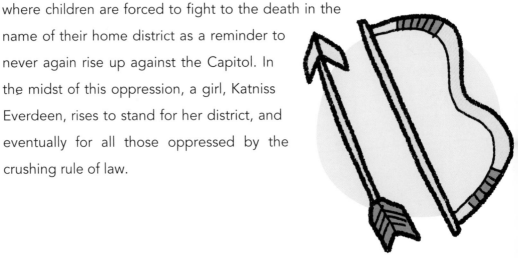

Books and Films

The Hunger Games—2008 (also a film released in 2012, rated PG-13)—Teenager Katniss Everdeen volunteers to enter the Hunger Games to save her sister who is chosen, and must use all her skill as a hunter to survive.

Catching Fire—2009 (also a film released in 2013, rated PG-13)—As a rebellion against the oppressive government begins to take hold and spread, Katniss and her friend and fellow victor Peeta Mellark once again have to fight in the Hunger Games.

Mockingjay—2010 (also two films released in 2014 and 2015, both rated PG-13)—Katniss becomes the unwitting leader of the rebellion against the oppressive government with hopes of creating a peaceful and prosperous world.

This series is intended for YA readers, but the intensity of the action and the scenes of children being forced to fight each other against their will makes this **a story for mature tweens or teens**.

DISTRICTS OF PANEM

Want to emulate the futuristic royalty of the Capitol with a fashion show? Or would you like to pretend your favorite fishing hole is part of District 4? The world of Panem is at your fingertips!

 The Capitol: Home to the Elite and Upper Classes

 District 7: Lumber

District 1: Luxury Goods

 District 8: Textiles

District 2: Masonry

 District 9: Grain

District 3: Technology

 District 10: Livestock

District 4: Fishing

 District 11: Agriculture

District 5: Power (Energy)

District 12: Mining

District 6: Transportation

District 13: The Lost District— Graphite and Nuclear Weapons

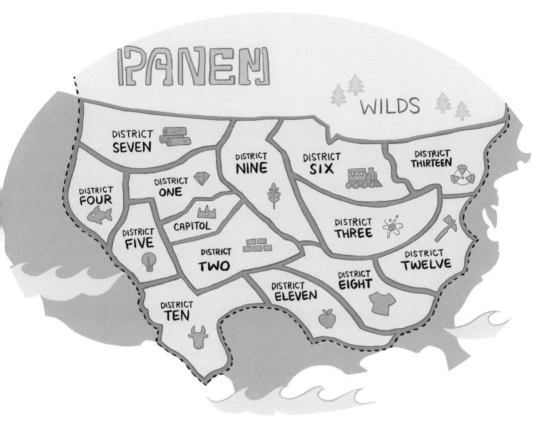

THE X-FILES

The truth is out there.

Created by Chris Carter and running for nine seasons from 1993 to 2002, *The X-Files* was arguably the most popular science fiction TV series at the time. FBI Special Agents Fox Mulder and Dana Scully investigated X-Files—cases that fell outside the purview of regular investigation because of some unknown, possibly paranormal element to the case. Sometimes scary and a bit dark, **this series is for teenagers or older**. Fox Mulder is a true believer in the paranormal and investigates each case with an unwavering focus on discovering unknown truths about the existence of extraterrestrial life, paranormal activity, and secret government conspiracies.

His partner, Dana Scully, is a scientist, a medical doctor, and ever the skeptic when it comes to all things paranormal and unknown.

Do you believe?

The tension between the characters and the personal relationship that grew over the nine seasons captivated a wide audience for a decade.

Films

There have been two films made from the series:

The X-Files—1998—PG-13—In a continuation of the TV series's themes, the FBI tries to separate Mulder and Scully before they dig too deep into a secret government cover-up and discover too much.

The X-Files: I Want To Believe—2008—PG-13—After many long years, the team is brought back together when a series of strange events threatens to cause a potentially global disaster that only Mulder and Scully can stop.

An additional tenth season revived *The X-Files* franchise in 2016, and the eleventh season premiered in January 2018. There is even talk of a third film, and all the original actors are said to be on board for filming, so stay tuned. The truth is out there!

Fan Favorite Episodes:

"Colony/End Game"—season 2, episodes 16,17—Mulder and Scully face off against a deadly alien bounty hunter in this groundbreaking season finale.

"The Post-Modern Prometheus"—season 5, episode 5—In a black-and-white homage episode to classic horror films, Mulder and Scully track down a Frankenstein-like monster created as the result of an experiment. A great introduction to the series for new beginners.

"Jose Chung's from Outer Space"—season 3, episode 20—One the best episodes to perfectly juggle science fiction and self-aware comedy, this episode tells the story of one alien abduction told from two points of view in a Rashomon-style approach with a comedic twist.

MYSTERY SCIENCE THEATER 3000

"Initiate show open!"

—MYSTERY SCIENCE THEATER 3000

A rarity in the science fiction genre, this comedy series follows the simple premise of three audience members watching science fiction B movies and making humorous comments about them while they watch. The fans get to enjoy these lesser, public domain films while listening to comic writers make fun of each film's flaws. Many of the films they watch are considered to be some of the worst films ever made.

Starting in 1988, *Mystery Science Theater 3000* ran for seven seasons on Comedy Central. It was then picked up by the Syfy Channel and ran for another three seasons.

Another sixty episodes were produced in 1995, and then fourteen more episodes ran for an eleventh season in 2015. There was also a film

made from the series in 1996 and a 2017 Netflix series revival, **all of which are appropriate for PG viewers**.

The show follows a janitor who has been trapped on a satellite orbiting Earth. He builds two robots to be his companions, and together they watch these films, commenting as they play. The resulting show had a narrow but avid fan base. The show's popularity grew widely, eventually being considered by some to be one of the best television shows ever created.

Fan Favorite Episodes:

"Space Mutiny"—episode 820—With a muscled action hero who can barely act leading this impressive flop of a film, Mike and his robot friends have no shortage of riffs to make this film hilarious.

"Werewolf"—episode 904—From bad accents to bad costumes to bad line delivery, this master of a bad film is cause for some great lines by the watchers, in what would otherwise be an unwatchable film.

"Pod People"—episode 303—With terrible production quality and a probable late addition of an E.T.-like character, this film is truly awful, but of course made great by the quips of the crew.

"Time Chasers"—episode 821—This take on *Back to the Future* is bad but watchable for its mock value all on its own, but when the boys get ahold of it, it becomes a masterpiece.

"Future War"—episode 1004—A martial artist space slave lands on Earth and is pursued by robots. Yup. The boys have a field day with this gem of a film, and the result is brilliant.

GAMES & GAMING

THOUGH VIDEO GAMES HAD EXISTED
since the 1950s, it wasn't until the 1970s that
they took off in arcades across the country. With
their large, stand-up computer screens, simple
buttons, and joysticks, these coin-operated
arcade games became hugely popular for
the young generation. The first commercially
successful video game, *Pong*, was released
in 1972, but the height of arcade games'
popularity was from 1978 to 1982, featuring such classic games as *Pac-Man*, *Galaga*,
Asteroids, *Defender*, *Space Invaders*, *Frogger*,
and *Donkey Kong*. In the early 1980s, Atari and
Intellivision introduced the first video gaming

consoles that could be played at home, sparking a video gaming industry that has been advancing and expanding ever since.

Tabletop games have recently seen a great resurgence in popular culture, but they have actually existed for millennia. "Tabletop games" include board games, dice games, card games, and role-playing games that involve moving

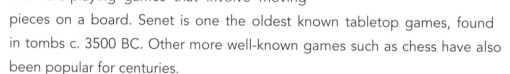

pieces on a board. Senet is one the oldest known tabletop games, found in tombs c. 3500 BC. Other more well-known games such as chess have also been popular for centuries.

Board game popularity in the United States waxes and wanes with the times, historically resurging in times of distress. Notably, America's most popular board game, Monopoly, was published during the Great Depression. Recently, board games are being repopularized by the German-style game or "Eurogame," a genre ignited by the 1995 publication of the Settlers of Catan. Eurogames are designed to be more elegant both in gameplay (more accessible to nongamers) and manufacturing (typically made of wood and sturdy cardboard rather than plastic), and aim to have all players engaged at all times.

Play is an essential human activity, and there are so many ways to use gaming to engage with your kids. Try out some of the following recommended games!

NINTENDO

Released in 1985, the Nintendo Entertainment System (NES) was an instant hit and revitalized the video game industry. Selling over sixty million units, the NES let people play games like *Mario* and *Zelda* in their homes for the first time. Nintendo arguably revolutionized home gaming, from the NES to such classics new and old as the Game Boy, SNES, Nintendo 64, Nintendo GameCube, Nintendo DS, and the Nintendo Switch.

Throughout all of Nintendo's games, there are common characters and themes. Some popular games we recommend are:

Super Mario Bros.—Mario travels through the Mushroom Kingdom to rescue Princess Toadstool from bad guy Bowser.

Metroid—Fly around in your ship and fight off Space Pirates who try to harness the power of the Metroids.

The Legend of Zelda—Play as the warrior Link, rescue Princess Zelda, and save the Kingdom of Hyrule from the clutches of the evil Ganon.

Donkey Kong—Jump from platform to platform as you dodge various obstacles in one of the most popular video games of all time.

Final Fantasy—*Final Fantasy* is considered one of the greatest role-playing video games (RPGs) ever made, and it is appropriate for a slightly more mature player.

POKÉMON

Beginning as only two handheld video games, *Pokémon* is now the highest grossing media franchise of all time. The brand has spread across almost every conceivable platform for two decades, with no sign of stopping.

Nintendo first released *Pokémon* for the Game Boy in 1996. The first generation of the game introduced the concepts of capturing, training, battling, and trading Pokémon creatures. Several generations of the game came out in the following years as the game became more popular and technology improved. On the twentieth anniversary of the franchise in 2016, Nintendo released *Pokémon Go*, a hugely popular augmented reality game for mobile devices. Nintendo also released two seventh-generation Pokémon games for the Nintendo 3DS, *Pokémon Sun* and *Pokémon Moon*. By this time, the total number of Pokémon was 802.

To this day, the notably low-tech *Pokémon* Trading Card Game remains popular around the world. Just like in the handheld games, players of the trading card game (TCG) assume the role of a trainer pitting the skill of their Pokémon against their rival's. The win conditions of the TCG are slightly different from the battles in the handheld games, but the essence is the same.

The *Pokémon* franchise also includes TV shows and movies. The *Pokémon* animated television series, which started in 1998 and is still running today, focuses on a young boy named Ash who befriends a Pokémon named Pikachu. Together they travel the world, battle other Pokémon, and work their way through many adventures.

Gotta Catch 'Em All Hide-and-Seek

In the mobile app *Pokémon Go*, you can find Pokémon in the real world and virtually catch in the app. To introduce Pokémon to your kids, you could adapt this game into a real-world hide-and-seek activity.

Materials

- Paper
- Colored pencils or markers
- Cardboard or poster board (optional)

1 Print out or draw illustrations of Pokémon creatures on paper, cardboard, or poster board. Depending on the age of your child, they may want to help you make the Pokémon before hiding. Gotta craft 'em all!

2 Hide papers folded up in small spaces (like pokéballs!), or get fancy with cardboard and hide standing, life-size Pokémon cutouts.

Once all Pokémon are hidden, let the games begin! You can now play with your child of any age by seeking out the Pokémon you have created and hidden yourselves! Give them a set limit to up the ante, or make them a scavenger hunt list with clues about their whereabouts.

XBOX

First introduced in 2001 and created by Microsoft, Xbox is currently one of the most popular gaming systems on the market today. The second generation, Xbox 360, was released in 2005 and was considered a huge leap forward in gaming technology. The current console, Xbox One, was released in 2013 and is among the most advanced gaming systems in the world.

Among the most popular game series for Xbox are:

For mature audiences:	For kids of all ages:
Halo	Fruit Ninja
Destiny	Peggle 2
Titanfall	FIFA Soccer
Fallout 4	Disney Infinity 3.0
Forza Motorsport	Lego Marvel Superheroes

PLAYSTATION

Launched in 1994 by Sony, the original PlayStation video game console was a tremendous commercial success. Then in 2000, the next generation, PlayStation 2, became the bestselling home video game console ever made. PlayStation 3 was released in 2006, and was also a great success. PlayStation 4 was released in 2013. It sold over a million units in the first twenty-four hours of its release, making it the fastest-selling video game console of all time.

Some of the games that have made the console so popular are:

For mature audiences	For kids of all ages:
The Last of Us	*Little Big Planet*
Grand Theft Auto	*Skylanders*
Resident Evil	*Lego Pirates of the Caribbean*
Red Dead Redemption	*Cars 2: The Video Game*
Tony Hawk's Pro Skater	*Lego Harry Potter*

All the mature games listed except for *Tony Hawk* have some fairly adult content and can in some situations get pretty dark. The "kids" games can be fun for kids and adults alike!

MINECRAFT: GATEWAY TO PC GAMES

Created by Markus Persson and developed by Mojang in 2009, this creative building game lets players construct their own worlds with 3D cubes. Now owned by Microsoft, *Minecraft* is hugely popular, selling over 121 million copies across multiple platforms by 2017. It's the second bestselling video game of all time, behind only *Tetris*.

The game is seen as a refreshing departure from almost all other games, giving players a tremendous amount of freedom to choose their activities and giving them no specific goals to accomplish, other than to simply survive, when playing in survival mode.

Minecraft is great for all ages, because of its peaceful options for play and lack of graphic violence. *Minecraft* also has a creative mode, where players have access to all the areas and resources of the game; they can build and explore, but they don't have to protect or feed themselves to survive.

Minecraft can be a great beginning for future gamers; they can get accustomed to role-playing and survival in this kid-friendly and adaptable world. As they get used to the game, they could try out other survival games such as *Lost in Blue* and *Subnautica*.

SETTLERS OF CATAN

A board game designed by Klaus Teuber and published in 1995, *Settlers of Catan* enjoys huge popularity in a world dominated by video and computer games. Players build settlements and roads by spending resources they collect according dice rolls, and the first player to reach a certain number of victory points wins.

Settlers of Catan is almost single-handedly responsible for what gamers are calling the second golden age of tabletop gaming. It has sold more than eighteen million copies worldwide and has been translated into more than thirty languages. It's even credited with converting the most reticent, game-averse friends and family members to devoted board games fans.

For nongamers, learning to play can be a steep but short learning curve, so while the **content is suitable for all ages, the explanation of the rules will be the biggest barrier for young kids**. As with any game, the key to a good time is preparedness. Make sure you read and thoroughly understand the rules of a new board game before playing so you're able to answer any questions about gameplay like a pro, and your kids will be hooked!

If you're a fan of *Settlers of Catan*, try these other world-building board games!

Risk

Bohnanza

7 Wonders

Ticket to Ride

Railways of the World

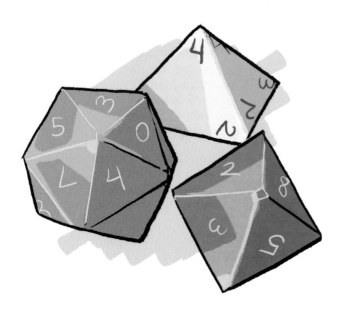

DUNGEONS & DRAGONS (D&D)

Perhaps the greatest role-playing game of all time is also considered to be the first. Co-created by Gary Gygax and Dave Arneson and published in 1974, Dungeons & Dragons is widely thought to be the first modern fantasy game ever created. The game was inspired by miniature wargames and a game called Chainmail, which was popular at the time.

Dungeons & Dragons uses several multiple-sided dice and allows its players to delve deeply into the roles of the characters they play. Players create characters in great detail, from species to abilities. They also often use miniature figurines to represent their characters' movements on grids, but this is not strictly necessary for play.

In its essence, D&D is an imaginative role-playing game that's appropriate for **all ages**, but a key component to a smooth campaign is a knowledgeable Dungeon Master (DM) who can take you through all the ins and outs of building a character and operating in your chosen campaign setting. If you are not a seasoned DM, don't fret! Local game stores often have open game nights where you and your kids can participate in campaigns run by experts, until you become an expert yourself!

LARPING

Bringing your favorite fantasy characters to life. Isn't that the ultimate fun for a truly devoted fan? Live action role-playing, or LARPing, has enjoyed a huge rise in popularity over the years. At Renaissance faires and other LARPing events around the world, participants dress up in costumes as ornate and accurate as their imaginations and wallets allow, and they actually act out the behaviors of their characters in real life alongside others who are doing the same.

LARPing is as old as costumed play itself, but the true LARP clubs were first organized in the late 1970s, no doubt inspired by the popularity of Dungeons & Dragons at the time. The role-playing aspect is similar, but LARPing differs from D&D in that you act your character's actions yourself, rather than conduct the campaign entirely in your party's collective imagination, as in D&D.

Today LARP clubs can be found everywhere and for every genre of fantasy and science fiction, and Renaissance faires are a common seasonal attraction for thousands of fans every year. They're great fun for all ages and a great way for all to play together!

RECOMMENDED GAMING: CLASSICS FOR KIDS

While all of the games already listed in this chapter are great, don't forget about the classics!

Monopoly	Clue
Chess	Life
War	Sorry!
Battleship	Stratego
Scrabble	

And don't forget how important it is to have a family game night. Think about how awesome it would be to get the whole family together, put your phones away, and play a board or card game together while talking, competing, and laughing all the while. In this day and age, it can be difficult to get the whole family to sit down together all at once, but if you find the right games, games that interest and entertain everyone, you will have some eager participants who will never want to miss a family game night!

CULT CLASSICS IN FILM & TELEVISION

THERE ARE SO MANY MORE AREAS OUT THERE WORTHY OF nerdy exploration with your kids, and each one can fill the pages of several books on their own! The following shows, movies, and series are selections considered pivotal to the nerd experience, and while they didn't appear in the other chapters, no nerd overview would complete without a nod in their direction.

E.T. The Extra-Terrestrial—1982—PG—Groundbreaking for its time, as are so many of Steven Spielberg's films, *E.T. The Extra-Terrestrial* is about a lovable and peaceful little alien who wants to find his way home and enlists the help of some very adventurous kids. This film is appropriate for ages ten and up.

The Goonies—1985—PG—In this Spielberg childhood adventure, a group of misfit kids hunt for buried treasure and end up having to battle the bad guys who are also on its trail. This film is also appropriate for ages ten and up.

Teenage Mutant Ninja Turtles—1984—G—Through mutagen ooze, anthropomorphic turtles come to life as teenage ninjas led by their rat sensei. Starting as a comic book series in 1984, the franchise broke out into numerous television and film series that enjoyed great popularity due to the wisecracking pack of teen turtles. In the *TMNT* comic books, movies, and TV show, the action is fast and entertaining and the lessons are about morality, family, and loyalty. The franchise is appropriate for kids ages ten and up.

Indiana Jones—1981, 1984, 1989, 2008, and 2020—PG and PG-13—The signature fedora and whip can bring to mind only one man: Indiana Jones. Another Spielberg creation starting with *Raiders of the Lost Ark* in 1981, the charismatic anthropologist adventurer Indiana Jones captured the imaginations of audiences worldwide and led to a franchise and following that is still strong today. With sometimes more mature themes, these films are for young teens or mature preteens.

Tron—1982—PG—In *Tron*, a computer programmer is transported inside the video game software he developed, where he has to battle for his life in the very games he created. Director film Steven Lisberger says *Tron* was inspired from the video game *Pong*. Appropriate for most audiences, this film enjoys a smaller but intense cult following, and it inspired a sequel years later.

Back to the Future—1985—PG—Not only does teenager Marty McFly face all the normal troubles of high school, but he also is trusted back in time when his lovable old friend, the mad scientist Doc, creates a time machine that malfunctions. Marty is sent back to the 1950s when his parents were school-mates. The '50s set with the '80s mindset makes for great entertainment, and the film led to two sequels. This film is appropriate for most audiences.

Sherlock—Four seasons, 2010–Present—The BBC produced a modern-day version of Sir Arthur Conan Doyle's classic detective series *Sherlock Holmes*. Structured in four short seasons in miniseries form, these stories pitted the consulting detectives against the most brilliant criminal minds ever created for the screen. The interplay between the two main characters is great fun. This show is for slightly more mature audiences, not only because of the subject matter but also the cerebral nature of the scripts.

Buffy the Vampire Slayer—Seven seasons, 1997–2003—Created by Joss Whedon, a cult hero for the brilliant worlds and characters he creates, *Buffy the Vampire Slayer* is filled with quirky dialogue and well-paced stories. First released as a film in 1992 to limited critical success, *Buffy the Vampire Slayer* saw its cult following explode with the television series that ran from 1997 to 2003. This show is for slightly more mature audiences because of the themes and occasional violence, as evidenced in the title.

Firefly—One season, 2002–2003—Another triumph of Joss Whedon, this space adventure story with a western feel combines action, science fiction, and Whedon's great ability for quirky and quick dialogue. The year is 2517 and humans inhabit a new star system divided by a civil war. The crew of the ship *Serenity*, on the losing side of the war, scrapes together a living as adventurous outlaws. Released in 2002 to huge fan adoration but poor commercial success, the series was canceled after fourteen episodes were produced. It is still widely considered one of the greatest tragedies in popular culture. Both the television show and the following film *Serenity* are for more mature audiences given the action, violence, and occasional adult themes.

Dune—published in 1965 (also a film released in 1984, rated PG-13)—This science fiction novel became a lasting cult classic, and it was made into a film in 1984 with many spin-off stories, comics, and video games. Intelligent and complex with political undertones, this story is for teen audiences and older.

Alien—1979—R—This science fiction horror classic directed by Ridley Scott pits a female hero, Ellen Ripley, against a virtually unstoppable alien that has infiltrated her ship, leaving no one else alive. This film was groundbreaking for its time, and is appropriate only for mature audiences.

Predator—1987—R—Cinema powerhouse Arnold Schwarzenegger leads a team of elite soldiers through the jungle on a mission where he encounters more than the enemy he is expecting: a monster from an alien race of hunters who is picking off his team members for sport. This film is for adult audiences only.

CONCLUSION: THE SECRET TO CONTAGIOUS ENTHUSIASM WITH YOUR KIDS

Sharing science fiction and fantasy stories that held such importance for you growing up is a great way to bond with your child. It's a gift that's meaningful and lasting, and most important of all, it's a way to connect with your child—to talk, to play, to share.

And for the Nerdy Parent, there is no better way to rediscover the greatness of these stories than to share that love with your kids. One of the greatest experiences of parenthood is being able to bond with your child by engaging in activities that are meaningful to you both.

Often times a show of love can be through sharing a common interest. Share what you love with your kids, and show them how epic these worlds are and how awesome the characters are that come from them. Show them that these great and deeply enjoyable aspects of their childhood can become a part of their lives forever by showing them how meaningful they still are to you. So share the love and geek out with your kids. They'll thank you for it when they themselves are geek parenting someday.

KITSAP REGIONAL LIBRARY
www.krl.org

SILVER

3 9068 02964 3519

RAISE THE **COOLEST NERD**
THE WORLD HAS EVER KNOWN!

IN A WORLD filled with superheroes, wizards, spaceships, and magical telephone booths, who isn't a part of a fandom? This practical and comical guide is for the parents who want to share their fantastical interests with their children in hopes that they, too, will grow up to become little nerds.

With essential guides to FANTASY, COMIC BOOKS, GAMING CULTURE, **AND MORE**, engage your little ones with crafts, games, and recipes themed to their new nerdy interests—all with recommended reading lists and movie maps!

Learn the best possible way to ease kids into some of the murkier age-appropriate areas—ensuring no fears, just fun!—all to reach the goal of a shared passion for you and your child to explore together. Whether you want to raise a well-versed wizard or a caped crusader, *The Nerdy Parent's Guide* will ensure your quest succeeds!

S sourcebooks
sourcebooks.com

Parenting $16.99 U.S.
ISBN-13: 978-1-4926-6020-0

51699

9 781492 660200

EAN